Interviewing for Ra

'This is
to the fu
Sue Lav

'This is
tips botl
Sue Ma

Intervieu
the radi
response
recordir
ation, ar

Intervieu
porates
and exp
produce

Written
includes

- the l
- prac
- case
  diffi
- a dis
- a glc
  tenir

Jim Beaman is senior lecturer in radio journalism at The Surrey Institute of Art and Design, University College, and has worked as an instructor at BBC Radio Training. His broadcasting experience includes presenting, reporting and producing for BBC radio.

Media Skills

SERIES EDITOR: RICHARD KEEBLE
CITY UNIVERSITY, LONDON, UK
SERIES ADVISERS: WYNFORD HICKS, JENNY MCKAY
NAPIER UNIVERSITY, SCOTLAND

The *Media Skills* series provides a concise and thorough introduction to a rapidly changing media landscape. Each book is written by media and journalism lecturers or experienced professionals, and is a key resource for a particular industry. Offering helpful advice and information and using practical examples from print, broadcast and digital media, as well as discussing ethical and regulatory issues, *Media Skills* books are essential guides for students and media professionals.

Also in this series:

English for Journalists, 2nd edition
Wynford Hicks

Writing for Journalists
Wynford Hicks with Sally Adams and Harriett Gilbert

Producing for the Web
Jason Whittaker

Find more details of current *Media Skills* books and forthcoming titles at **www.producing.routledge.com**

Interviewing for Radio

Jim Beaman

London and New York

First published 2000
by Routledge
11 New Fetter Lane, London EC4P 4EE

Simultaneously published in the USA and Canada
by Routledge
29 West 35th Street, New York, NY 10001

Routledge is an imprint of the Taylor & Francis Group

© 2000 Jim Beaman

Typeset in Goudy Oldstyle and Scala Sans by Taylor & Francis Books Ltd
Printed and bound in Great Britain by Biddles Ltd, Guildford and King's Lynn

British Library Cataloguing in Publication Data
A catalogue record for this book is available from the British Library

Library of Congress Cataloging in Publication Data
Beaman, Jim, 1959–
Interviewing for radio / Jim Beaman.
Includes bibliographical references and index.
1. Interviewing on radio. I. Title.

PN1991.8.I57 B43 2000
791.44'028–dc21   00–025457

ISBN 0–415–22909–X (hb)
ISBN 0–415–22910–3 (pb)

Contents

Preface   vii

1   The birth of the radio interview   1

2   The role and purpose of the radio interview   6

3   Guidelines   19

4   Advice from the experts   43

5   Technical advice   52

6   Before the interview   64

7   At the interview   85

8   After the interview   132

9   Analysis of interviews   148

10   Information   156

Glossary   165

Index   171

Preface

Experienced radio interviewers may not find much of interest or of practical use within these pages. Hopefully, they will be able to nod sagely when they come across a good bit of advice or read about experiences similar to their own. To become a good radio interviewer there is no substitute for experience, but we all have to start somewhere. Like many others, I learnt the pleasures and pitfalls of interviewing by actually doing it. In those early days working in news and programme production, I welcomed any guidance and feedback about my performance from more experienced broadcasters. The problem with experience is that you can slip into bad habits, so I think it is important to be humble enough to encourage honest feedback from those whose judgement you trust, even if you feel you can do the job blindfold.

The aim of this book is to act as a form of support and a guide to good practice for the journalist who is trying to develop their skill in the art of interviewing for radio. There are no startling revelations, nor many hard-and-fast rules, but there is plenty of advice. Many of the words of wisdom contained within are based on the experiences of professional colleagues in radio, radio training and education. You will no doubt discover what works for you, and you will develop your instincts and apply your own tricks of the trade.

This book is about interviewing for radio, and draws no distinction between interviewing for news and interviewing for programmes, except for particular procedures. In the same way, it draws no distinction between a journalist who interviews for news and one who interviews for programmes. All interviews broadcast are the product of journalism, be they about an issue of national importance or simply for entertainment. Anyone conducting an interview for broadcast, be they from the newsroom and considering themselves a serious journalist, or the presenter of the mid-morning show who prefers to think of themselves as an entertainer, applies the same ethical and professional considerations to their work.

Some trainee journalists are naturally anxious about meeting people and having to ask them questions. One trainee told me he was so nervous when he went to conduct his first interview that he forgot to shake hands with his interviewee. Some trainee journalists worry about the sound of their own voice, or whether they look as though they know what they are doing when the time comes to start operating their recording equipment, or whether their questions sound stupid, or whether they are asking the right questions; they worry about what the interviewee will think of them, what other journalists covering the same story will think of their performance, and how they will cope when things go wrong. They want to know how to overcome their fear of cold-calling complete strangers on the telephone, how to tell their editor that the vox-pop subject they were sent to record interviews about was a waste of time because the only replies they collected from the public were 'who cares?', and how to stop an interviewee from talking too much.

I hope this book will help provide some of the knowledge they require to develop confidence and a positive attitude, and alleviate some of their anxieties about interviewing a complete stranger.

Interviewing for radio is challenging, exciting and life-enriching, so try to enjoy it.

1

The birth of the radio interview

Radio broadcasting in the UK began in 1922, but for many years the interview was an ignored resource. Newspapers and cinema newsreels used interviews as a method of eliciting news and when covering stories, but radio did not. In the early days of radio broadcasting, speech output mainly consisted of talks, speeches, commentaries and reports. News broadcasts were made up of text compiled from material provided by news agencies. They did not contain any voice reports or interview clips.

So when and how did the broadcast interview make its appearance on the UK airwaves? Archive records can tell us the date and location of the first radio outside broadcast, and when an election address was first broadcast, and when the news was first read by a woman, but not who conducted the first broadcast interview on radio, what the topic under discussion was, nor who the interviewee was. If there were such things as interviews, then nobody felt that they were important enough to archive or to keep the details on record.

Interviews did eventually start making their presence felt, but it was a painstaking progression that seemed to stumble into being, and involved the bringing together of the pioneering groundwork of a number of broadcasters working in different parts of the BBC.

The edition of the *BBC Handbook* that looks back on 1931 and reports on performance and developments in radio broadcasting during that year sheds some light on how speech radio, particularly in the Talks Department, was beginning to at least allow discussion between people with a diversity of views to be heard on the air. A chapter headed 'The important symposiums' reveals:

> When the ban on controversy was lifted by the Postmaster-General, the BBC made their earliest experiments in the form of discussions and debates.

The chapter goes on to describe how:

> The 'dogfight' method has advantages for straight and simple issues in which there is a clear pro and con; and conversational discussion between two or three people is useful for conveying good talk of an after-dinner kind.

A few years later the mainstay of the Talks Department, the radio discussion, underwent a significant change. The impromptu unscripted debates broadcast in the early days tended to be meandering, sometimes unintelligible discussions between eminent professors with constant interruption and deviation by the participants, so the BBC decided to introduce an experienced broadcaster to join them in front of the microphone to act as an umpire, to steer the debate and to make sense of it all without actually taking part in the discussion. Later, as the potential of this technique was developed, the studio chairman evolved into an interviewer asking the questions that would shape and focus the discussion.

During the 1930s, until after the Second World War, nearly all speech on radio was live and had to be pre-scripted. It could be argued that at least with a script you could guarantee something would be said. There was, and still is, always the risk that those not used to being interviewed would freeze when their moment came to speak. Programmes like *Standing on the Corner*, presented by Michael Standing, and *In Town Tonight* broadcast from the streets of London and, in the case of the latter, also from Heathrow Airport, achieved an extra edge because many answers provided by interviewees were spontaneous.

However, most of the voices that were heard on air were those of the upper middle class speaking standard southern English. According to the programme *They Did It First*, broadcast in 1981, in the early days of broadcasting in the 1920s the BBC's first Director General, John Reith, declared that only those 'qualified to speak' should be heard on the radio. Inevitably, speakers were chosen from the great men of the day; certainly no women were chosen as they were deemed not to have suitable voices for radio. The general public, it seems, were welcome to be listeners but, in Reith's view, not worthy enough to be listened to.

Another extract from the 1931 *Handbook* illustrates the way BBC programme makers and editorial decision makers were making their choices of speakers to participate in future broadcasts.

> Few things are more illuminating or more refreshing than to hear points of view not often expressed – the views of ordinary men and women whose claim to speak is just that their experience is that of thousands of others.
>
> (221)

Social documentary programmes like *'Opping 'Oliday*, produced by Lawrence Gilliam and broadcast on the BBC's London Regional in 1934, were the first to allow ordinary people to speak for themselves on air. 'Now they speak, via an interviewer for the microphone', are the words used in the introduction to the programme. Researchers wrote down their words, sometimes edited or re-wrote them, and then the original 'actuality speakers' rehearsed the scripts and spoke their words into the microphone – the result was often a stilted and performed witness account. Listening to the rushes of *'Opping 'Oliday* featured in the programme *They Did It First*, which explores the techniques of the early documentary makers, the interviewers, although friendly, show their lack of experience by making the basic mistake of doing most of the talking. They have the excuse of carrying out pioneering work; today's broadcasters do not.

In the programme *They Speak for Themselves*, also highlighted in *They Did It First*, producer Olive Shapley describes how, when preparing material for a section on holidays in Blackpool, she preferred to 'gather raw interviews not scripted or read', and claimed that it was the 'easiest thing in the world over a cup of tea'. Great store was made during the introduction to the broadcast of programmes such as *Canal Journey*, again produced by Olive Shapley, by the fact that 'all you will hear was made without script or rehearsal'.

Interviews with 'real' people sat more comfortably in the documentary formats of the 1930s that chose not to use the scripted formula. One example is a feature programme entitled *Speed the Plough* broadcast in

September 1938, covering a ploughing competition at Moreton-in-Marsh. This effective and charming piece uses commentary and interviews with the local organisers, judges and the winner of the competition. Sidney Carter and David Gretton present, interview and commentate with enthusiasm and expertise, and without once sounding patronising towards the subject or the people involved. Their questioning of obviously virgin interviewees is friendly, good-humoured, direct and relevant:

- As a judge what are you looking for?
- What's wrong with this particular furrow?
- What's the difference in technique between ploughing with horses and using a tractor?

The answers they receive sound natural and unrehearsed.

In 1936 Richard Dimbleby, who was trying to persuade the BBC to give him a position as a 'news observer', suggested that rather than rely on agencies, the BBC should have its own reporters/correspondents to cover major news stories. Their job would be to write their own accounts of an event and also find an eyewitness to describe what they saw or did. He believed that the news bulletins needed a bit of life injected into them. But the idea of using location interviews in news bulletins was not seized upon, and it was several years before it was put into practice. The National Sound Archive at the British Library holds examples of the BBC Sound Archive, which contains possibly one of the earliest recordings of a topical interview which may have been used in a news bulletin. It is a seemingly dull conversation between Dimbleby and Captain G. J. Powell on his record-breaking transatlantic flight in September 1937. The seemingly lacklustre interview lasts one and a half minutes, with many of the Captain's answers sounding as though he were reading from a prepared script, together with two of Dimbleby's questions: 'Will you be making any more crossings this year?' and 'Was the flight an exciting one?'. These closed questions, luckily, did not elicit one-word replies.

Once News was separated from Talks during typical internal departmental wrangling, Dimbleby and others like him could try to exploit the world of sound and audio storytelling. Dimbleby, for example, is credited with producing the first radio package with a report that combined live links and pre-recorded actuality on discs with the in- and out-points marked with chalk.

As radio ownership increased over the years and the costs of buying a set came down, the social range of the radio audience widened, and the networks providing the programmes became more defined in their roles, each with its distinctive sound. The timid attitude of the BBC towards the development of broadcasting techniques was slow in changing. The combination of all the experiments in speech radio, together with the need of the listener for truthful and first-hand information, as well as the introduction of television, must have contributed to the acceptance of a more liberating and revealing form of communication, namely the radio interview. Once the position and purpose of the interview, and the roles and the selection of interviewer and interviewee were recognised by the broadcasters and the listeners, the potential of the radio interview was then established as a vital and indispensable mode of delivery in speech output. It can be live or recorded, probing or light-hearted; it can either stand alone or be harvested to provide a source of news and add credibility to programmes and features.

The interview has been for some time an essential and important part of radio broadcasting. Unlike the fickle fashions for TV chat shows, the radio interview has continued to find favour. There have been some developments, particularly in news interviewing: with the move towards pacier bulletins, the demand for soundbite clips has become the norm, and the practice of interviewing appointed correspondents for updates and analysis has increased and is fully exploited.

2

The role and purpose of the radio interview

In their newsgathering or programme-making activities, reporters, correspondents, producers and editors are looking to approach a story in three stages: to preview an event before it happens, to report an event as it is happening and to analyse an event once it has happened. They are also interested in an angle from which to approach their story. In choosing the angle they are looking for three ingredients within that story: topicality, human interest (about an individual or a group) and conflict (in words or in actions).

Radio news coverage has the advantage of speed and frequency. The listener can hear a reporter or contributor tell their story on air as an event is unfolding, via telephone, radio car or studio link to the newsroom and studio.

All radio output is made up of a combination of voices, sounds, music and pauses. In radio news the main contribution is usually made by voices, with the other audio providing the illustrative material or soundtrack. A major contribution to this output is the result of interviewing, be it for research purposes or actual broadcast. Live or recorded, lasting thirty seconds or thirty minutes, light or heavyweight, about an exclusive or well publicised story, the aim of the interview is to convey or check information, to give expert or general opinion, to explain or account for an action or a decision, to describe an emotion or feelings, or to give an insight into a person's personality or history. It offers the opportunity to hear the interviewee's own words, their tone of voice and characteristics of delivery. Is the speaker smiling as they talk or is their voice beginning to waver slightly as nervousness or emotion begins to influence their breathing? For the interviewee there is less chance that their words will be misinterpreted, because they are not being quoted but are telling the story directly to the listener, who can hear where they may place emphasis in a phrase.

The radio journalist interviews for the purpose of gathering relevant voices to illustrate a story for the listener, often a story that the listener will be able to relate to, perhaps even a shared experience. It can be said that the radio interview is a reflection of a temporary and short-term relationship between the person asking the questions and the person answering them. It is more than a conversation. A conversation relies on both parties paticipating in both questioning and answering. The roles in an interview are very clearly defined. One person asks and a second person answers. The person who asks should be the one with authoritative control, thus allowing them, when appropriate, to question and test the answers they glean from the interviewee.

From the listener's point of view it is not an accidentally overhead conversation, but a deliberate broadcast influencing their opinion or attitude, which they have chosen to access via the radio. What they hear should contribute to their understanding and aid them in any conclusions they wish to draw about what they have heard during the interview. They may also expect the interviewer to ask questions on their behalf; the questions that they would put themselves if they were face-to-face with the interviewee. However, the best question of all time is wasted if the answer it receives fails to hit the mark.

Interviewing is also a research process which is one step behind a news story that has already happened – the collection and confirmation of facts and the identity of those involved in the breaking and developing story. This method of gathering and confirming facts can also be the first stage in ascertaining the broadcasting ability of a potential interviewee.

WHAT CHANGES A WORKMANLIKE INTERVIEW INTO A MEMORABLE ONE?

- The on-air relationship between the interviewer and interviewee.
- An unexpected revelation by the interviewee.
- A revealing insight into a situation or personality.
- The provision of new information.

WHY DO PEOPLE AGREE TO BE INTERVIEWED ON THE RADIO?

- They can get free advertising or promotion for themselves, an organisation, a product, service or activity.

- They have to because it is part of their job definition as spokesperson for a company or department, or in their role as press officer on a committee.

- They need to set the record straight and end speculation.

- They want to balance the coverage by accentuating the positive in what appears to be a negative and damaging story.

- They feel the cathartic need to talk to someone. Even those involved in an incident can sometimes welcome the invitation to talk about their experience.

WHY DO PEOPLE DECLINE TO BE INTERVIEWED ON THE RADIO?

- They believe you intend to catch them out or humiliate them.

- They are afraid their views may be misrepresented.

- They think that you will change the meaning of what they say by editing the interview.

- They are not sure how they will come across on air.

- They don't like the sound of their own voice.

- They are nervous about what their colleagues, boss and family will say about their performance on air.

- They are too upset about what has happened and may also resent your presence.

If you think that you may be refused an interview, it may be prudent to have a second choice in mind. Your reluctant first choice may be only too happy to suggest a suitable alternative.

WHERE AND HOW ARE THE INTERVIEWS USED?

- News clip or cut – a short clip (a few seconds) of the interview used as part of a news bulletin.

- News interview – live or recorded short interview lasting 2–5 minutes as part of a longer programme.

- Two-way – a live or recorded interview within a programme between a studio-based programme presenter/interviewer and a fellow radio/TV reporter or correspondent who may act as an eyewitness or commentator.

- Taster – a short extract (a few seconds) of a longer recorded interview used as part of an illustrative menu at the start of a programme.

- Wrap – short clip or clips of the original recorded interview sandwiched between links written and read by a reporter or correspondent telling the story. Used within a news bulletin, a programme or a feature, a wrap lasts about thirty seconds to a minute or so.

- Package – similar to a wrap but usually longer and featuring selected extracts from one or more recorded interviews which may be pulled together from a range of sources and punctuated with illustrative sound effects, music, archives, etc., linked by a reporter or correspondent. Used as part of a programme a package can last between two and five minutes. They are often news-led, tend to take a logical form and are usually made and broadcast on the same day. A simple package could consist of two interview clips sandwiched between three links.

- Vox-pop – from the Latin *vox populi* (voice of the people). A series of snapshot opinions stitched together and usually lasting about 20–40 seconds. The interviewees are unnamed members of the public giving an answer to the same question. Recorded at random by a reporter, the finished product usually features just the voices of the interviewees.

- Feature – similar to a package but usually longer and containing more elements. They often stand alone rather than being featured as part of a programme. They can last from 5–30 minutes and may be produced as much by the imagination as by the subject matter.

- Montage – a feature or documentary that excludes a narrator or interviewer's voice and uses only the voices of interviewees and illustrative material to tell the story. Difficult but satisfying to produce. Challenging radio for the listener.

- Phone-ins – a phone-in will feature interviews with listeners and expert contributors if it is topical or discussion-based. Questions are invited from listeners to experts if it is an advice line phone-in. Vox-pops are sometimes used to kick off the discussion.

- Sequence/magazine programme – could include a combination of live and recorded interviews, vox-pops, phone-ins, packages, wraps and tasters, or may concentrate on one guest interviewee. Programmes can last from thirty minutes to three hours.

- Documentaries – an in-depth and crafted recorded programme of up to an hour's length which can feature numerous contributors and illustrative material.

CATEGORIES OF INTERVIEW

Before you can start asking your contributor any questions, it is important that you are aware of the different types of broadcast interview. Here are four categories of interview, but it should be remembered that an interview could be made up of a combination of all or some of them.

- Collecting information: The main purpose of this type of interview is to obtain facts or elucidation about a subject, and the interview can take place off- or on air. It will include interviews with experts, spokespersons or eyewitnesses. You need to make sure you are talking to the most knowledgeable person available, and to spend a fair amount of time going over the questions you are likely to ask, ensuring that the topic is covered in a clear and logical sequence.

- Expressing opinion or offering explanation: Once facts are made available, you need someone to interpret and comment on them for you and the listener. So once again you will be contacting your friendly expert on the subject, or the spokesperson from an organisation for reaction. You may also want a snapshot of opinion from the general public; this is usually in the form of a vox-pop or phone-in.

- Accountability: The aim of this interview is to ask someone responsible for decision making and instigating a plan to explain and justify their reasons for embarking on a course of action. As an interviewer you may need to challenge these actions, or invite comments from another interviewee who opposes or disagrees with the actions.

- Emotional or sensitive: For many journalists this type of interview is the most problematic. The knee-jerk cliché question they usually ask is 'How do you feel … ?' This is understandable because they are trying to explore the interviewee's state of mind – they may be a victim or a relative of a victim involved in a tragedy or a crime. On a lighter note, it may be the return of a round-the-world yachtsperson. Whatever the subject, interviews that will produce an emotional response need sensitive and non-intrusive questioning. Extra care should be taken in making the initial approach for an interview. It is advisable not to attempt to conduct an interview

(a)   until permission has been obtained from the potential interviewee;

(b)   if the person appears to be in a state of shock. The interview should describe or explain what happened, or contain information that would help others to avoid similar incidents in the future.

WHAT WORKS BEST ON RADIO?

- The cliché 'the pictures are better on radio' is only true if the words and sounds chosen to paint the picture are used effectively and stimulate the aural imagination.

- Facts, figures and generalities which are described and explained in a clear and imaginative way.

- Hearing about people's feelings, opinions and experiences directly from those involved.

WARM-UP EXERCISES TO GET YOU THINKING ABOUT WHAT YOU HEAR

- Switch on your radio and tune across the wavebands. Try to identify the stations you hear. Note how long you listened before you identified the station and what it was that you heard that helped you to name the station – a station identification jingle, the music selection, the voice of the presenter, or the style of the programming?

- If you were given the chance to interview one person, who would you choose? If you could ask them just one question, what would it be? How would you word or phrase the question to get the most detailed answer?

- Listen to a radio interview and write down the questions asked by the interviewer. What makes them effective or ineffective? Would you word them differently? Using the categories listed in this book, can you identify the category of interviewer and interview, where and how the interview was being used, why the interviewee was chosen for the interview and why they agreed, and what other sounds other than the voices of interviewer and interviewee were used to illustrate the interview?

- Compare the interviewing techniques used on *Desert Island Discs*, *In the Psychiatrist's Chair* and *Today*, which can all be heard on BBC Radio 4. What differences and similarities are evident to the listener in the way questions are asked on these programmes? Describe the style of interviewing. What is the purpose of the interview for each of these programmes?

- Select a story from a newspaper and imagine you are being sent out to conduct interviews for a radio programme on the same subject. Who would you choose to interview? Write down three questions you must ask your interviewee to get their side of the story. Try to work out what answers you are likely to get to your questions.

- Check through the radio pages of a listings magazine or newspaper and try to work out which programmes would feature interviews, the categories of interviews they would be likely to feature, and the range of interviewees you might hear. Give the programmes a listen and see if you were correct in your assumptions.

- Listen to a selection of news bulletins. Try to work out how much of what you hear has been generated by someone in the news team conducting an interview.

- Interview a friend or relative about a particular topic that they know something about. During the interview make notes based on their answers, but do not try to write everything down exactly as they say it. After the interview, try to convey as accurately as possible to a third party what your interviewee has been saying. Did you leave out anything crucial? Were you selective about the information that you passed on to the third party? Did you add any information that was not conveyed to you, but which you felt needed to be said to fill in gaps or support what was said originally?

THE ROLE OF THE INTERVIEWER

The interviewer's job is to act as a catalyst. To pose pertinent questions that will result in full, considered and concise answers that tell a story. It may also be necessary to ask seemingly impertinent questions that will draw appropriate and revealing answers from the interviewee. The interviewer is there to put the questions the listener would like to ask, and the questions the listener ought to ask. The personal qualities required by a radio interviewer include a natural inquisitiveness and the confidence that enables them to be persistent when questioning another person.

Quite often, however, the interviewer is faced with the uneasy task of covering a topic that is beyond their own experience, and may even be an issue that they have avoided because it is too painful or touches on their own unresolved feelings. Subjects that embarrass or scare the interviewer or interviewee are having to be confronted face-to-face. An interviewer must decide during the course of the interview whether to proceed with caution, or to take control by asking the questions that naturally arise.

Choosing the right interviewer is just as important as choosing the right interviewee. Matching the two people correctly will determine a successful outcome in the resulting interview. Much will depend on the perspective the final interview will take on a topic. If the role of a radio programme or item within a programme is to give a youth angle, show a subject from a woman's viewpoint or discuss a gay issue, then an interviewer will be chosen who can sympathetically cover it from that perspective. Interviewers sometimes complain about being typecast for particular interviews. British Asian journalists, for example, say they don't always want to be the one sent out on Asian stories or to get an Asian community view on a story. Some interviewers get a reputation for being good at live interviews or for producing humorous packages, or for being practised in the art of getting the sensitive interview, and then find they are being passed over if the subject is not in their usual field.

This means that they do not get the opportunity to expand their repertoire, or apply their acknowledged skills to a story and perhaps produce a different and even fresh approach to the line of questioning.

Listen carefully to a wide range of radio interviewers and think about why their particular techniques and style of interviewing work. Then imagine how they would have to adapt those techniques if they were interviewing for a different programme, station, or range of interviewees.

John Humphreys (BBC Radio 4's *Today*) is acknowledged as being one of the best political interviewers on radio with his brisk and probing style of questioning. John Dunn (recently retired from BBC Radio 2) made magazine-programme interviewing sound easy because he was genuinely interested in the people he spoke to and what they had to say. Jenny Murray (BBC Radio 4's *Woman's Hour*) has the ability to handle an extensive range of subjects and approaches within one programme, due to her wide experience as an interviewer and her sympathetic understanding of what makes people tick. High-profile interviewers like James Naughtie, Jimmy Young, Nicky Campbell and Sue Lawley are talked and written about as much as the people they interview, but there are plenty of broadcasters who don't hit the headlines or get their names mentioned during parliamentary debates who are worthy of your attention. Listen to interviews featured in news and programmes broadcast on BBC and independent local radio, the BBC's regional networks, community and even student and hospital radio if you can access them. The quality, techniques and revelations that emerge can be impressive.

In the radio programme *Invitation to Speak*, John Freeman, who had vast experience in both radio and TV interviewing, explained that 'television does most of the work for the interviewer by showing the interviewee's eyes and the sweat on their forehead, but with radio you have to dig out more'. According to Freeman, to be a good interviewer you have to be 'inquisitive about other people's business'. In the same programme, Robin Day insists that an interview should 'satisfy the enquiring mind of the listener' and that the interviewer should be 'forceful, polite, careful in phrasing of questions and treat the subject with respect'.

TYPES OF INTERVIEWER

If you want to be a good interviewer, you need to develop an individual style and approach to the way you ask questions. Remember that the radio listener will be interested in hearing the question as well as the answer. The golden rule is that good interviewers knows how to listen. They use what they hear to determine the questions that will be asked and the manner in which they are asked. When deciding what questions to ask, think about what answer you are likely to get from your interviewee, and decide if you are prepared to accept such an answer at face value or whether you will need to push a little harder to get a more satisfactory response. It helps if you have a good idea what the answer will be before you ask a question, but you should never reveal this knowledge to the listener in the way you put the question.

In the programme *I'm Glad You Asked Me That*, former Prime Minister Jim Callaghan said that he preferred 'the tougher interviewer, because the listening public end up feeling sympathetic towards the interviewee'. Norman Tebbit MP, in the same programme, said he felt that he 'responded better to the tough interviewer'.

What sort of interviewers do we hear regularly on radio? What sort of interviewer do we prefer? All interviewers have aspirations to be the best in their field, but flaws can develop as time goes by, a bit like the bad habits you pick up when you have been a qualified driver for a while. Regular monitoring of your performance by playing back recordings and listening to your interviews critically can help.

It is worth remembering that the word interview has other stressful connotations: attending a job interview, an interview with the bank manager and, of course, being interviewed by the police. An interview with a journalist can sometimes be as painful, embarrassing and just plain uncomfortable. Interviewees are often referred to as being 'grilled' or 'in the hot seat'.

There are also those who misconceive the role and image of the interviewer. If you want to create the wrong impression with your interviewee and listener, try adopting some of the following techniques:

- Flattery will get you everywhere. As long as the listener can hear you putting on a performance you can get away with appearing to be very interested in the interviewee before the interview and gushingly flattering on-air. But beware, your insincerity will be easy to see through and your interviewee will not give of their best for fear of sounding the same.

- If you want to get the better of your interviewee, then interrogation can unsettle them. If you are lucky, your interviewee will storm out mid-interview, thereby enhancing your image and reputation as a journalist to be reckoned with. Techniques you can use include: aggressively maintaining eye contact with the interviewee, shaking your head in disgust or despair when the interviewee speaks, and regularly interrupting mid-sentence.

Try not to scare off your contributor; you may want to interview them again. Even if you do have a reputation as a skilled interrogator, the chances are that the interviewee will be better prepared with answers and will not allow themselves to be provoked into over-reacting. You may end up with the reputation of being a counterfeit Robin Day or simply a paper tiger. Remember, not all interviews demand a challenging technique. Sometimes you may need to encourage your interviewee or investigate an issue. The interviewee is not your opponent, and an interview is not about point-scoring.

- Been there, done that: As an experienced interviewer you have seen and heard it all before. You probably did the same interview about the same subject at the same time last year. You have another half-dozen interviews to do today, so let's just get this one in the can.

As an interviewee it is much more difficult to respond to a bored interviewer than to a hectoring one, so they will probably slip into the same mood as the interviewer. The result is obvious. Try to see each interview, no matter how boring or unimportant it may be to you, as potentially the best one you will ever do.

- You pride yourself on your wide knowledge. You feel you know something about any subject under the sun. You believe that the more you can show what you know, the more impressed the interviewee and the listener will be. You pride yourself on the intelligence, length and complexity of the questions you ask. You love to hear an interviewee say on air 'Gosh! You have done your research. Where did you find that out?'. You also know where you stand on an issue because you took the time to make a judgement before the interview.

In fact your questions are long-drawn-out epistles full of facts and figures, academic analysis, personal opinion and a quote from a poet thrown in for good measure. You may feel justified in editorialising because you are well informed, but you may find you do not have all the evidence to qualify you to do so. Remember that you are not the most important person in the studio – this role belongs to the interviewee and you owe it to the listener to get the best out of your contributor.

- You haven't had time to do any research for this interview, but you have done so many before that it's like falling off a log. You think that you will ask better questions if you start from the point of knowing nothing. You may try to scan the press release to get the gist of a book during the news before your programme starts, but after all the author is here to tell you what it's all about.

You may get away with it. But quite often your questions will be over-long and painfully wordy because you are having to think as you speak and haven't worked out what to ask. Your style may be laidback and chatty but that is no excuse for laziness.

If you want to create an impression and make a career of interviewing, get a reputation for being a good listener, with the authority to ask questions on behalf of your audience as well as yourself.

- Acknowledge and accept that every interviewee has a point of view, and respect them for it.

- Develop an ability not only to see both sides of an argument but also to know the best way to challenge them if you have to act as devil's advocate. The listener should be aware of both sides of an argument before they can make up their minds about where they stand on an issue.

- Ask relevant questions and allow your interviewee time to answer.

- Give the impression you are listening by clever use of body language, and ask further questions based on previous replies.

- Ask carefully worded questions that are based on sound research, are factually correct and that investigate a topic and gently probe the thoughts of the interviewee.

- Know enough about the topic of the interview to be capable of asking informed questions and making sensible comments.

- Ensure the style and range of questioning is appropriate for the subject and the mood of the piece.

- Under critical analysis the interview should be seen to excel in its editorial content, production values and technical competence.

- The interview should appear to be over all too soon, but the impression is that the subject has been covered efficiently and fully.

THE ROLE OF THE INTERVIEWEE

An interviewee is often described as the guest, the contributor, and even the victim. All these words sum up the role they play when they are participating in an interview.

A good interviewee is worth their weight in gold to the interviewer. You are looking for a speaker who wants the interview to be as successful as you do. This means you want them to answer your questions and not go off at a tangent or put up an invisible barrier between the two of you.

Interviewees should be enthusiastic and knowledgeable about their subject without being obsessive to the point of being boring, and should be keen to get everyone else to understand their enthusiasm and be carried along with them. They should, when appropriate, be good storytellers and be prepared to sparkle on air.

The interviewee should be the right person to talk about a particular subject. Some organisations insist that it is the job of the chairperson to represent them in the media. Unfortunately they may be a good chairperson but it does not follow that they can communicate well with the listener.

The role of the interviewee is to get their message across and raise awareness, but at the same time to be aware of what it is that you need from the interview. To respond to questions posed by the interviewer, but not to expect the interviewer to do all the work. To respect the role of the interviewer and not show off by playing games such as making the interviewer work hard for the answers, or trying to give the listener the impression that the interviewer is ignorant by talking down to them.

3
Guidelines

THE NUJ CODE OF CONDUCT

In joining the National Union of Journalists you agree to abide by the Code of Conduct. The Code is designed to help develop and maintain the highest possible standards of professionalism.

What the Code says

1   A journalist has a duty to maintain the highest professional and ethical standards.

2   A journalist shall at all times defend the principles of the freedom of the press and other media in relation to the collection of information and the expression of comment and criticism. He/she shall strive to eliminate distortion, news suppression and censorship.

3   A journalist shall strive to ensure that the information he/she disseminates is fair and accurate, avoid the expression of comment and conjecture as established fact and falsification by distortion, selection or misrepresentation.

4   A journalist shall rectify promptly any harmful inaccuracies, ensure that corrections and apologies receive due prominence, and afford the right to reply to persons criticised when the issue is of sufficient importance.

5   A journalist shall obtain information, photographs and illustration only by straightforward means. The use of other means can be justified only by over-riding considerations of the public interest. The

journalist is entitled to exercise a personal conscientious objection to the use of such means.

6 Subject to justification by over-riding considerations of the public interest, a journalist shall do nothing which entails intrusion into private grief and distress.

7 A journalist shall protect confidential sources of information.

8 A journalist shall not accept bribes nor shall he/she allow other inducements to influence the performance of his/her professional duties.

9 A journalist shall not lend himself/herself to the distortion or suppression of the truth because of advertising or other considerations.

10 A journalist shall only mention a person's race, colour, creed, disability, illegitimacy, marital status (or lack of it), age, gender, or sexual orientation if this information is strictly relevant. A journalist shall neither originate nor process material which encourages discrimination on any of the above mentioned grounds.

11 A journalist shall not take advantage of information gained in the course of his/her duties, before the information is public knowledge.

12 A journalist shall not by way of statement, voice or appearance endorse by advertisement any commercial product or device save for the promotion of his/her own work or the medium by which he/she is employed.

INTERVIEWING ON THE BBC

In June 1990 the BBC issued a set of guidelines to staff entitled 'Interviewing on the BBC'. They were published following a series of complaints from politicians who were unhappy about the way they had been treated during interviews by journalists on some radio and television programmes. Politicians accused interviewers of being confrontational and discourteous. The interviewers complained that politicians were evasive and manipulative. The guidelines were intended to 'encourage sharp and considered, but always courteous' interviewing on the BBC.

In summary they stated:

• Programme editors are responsible for devising systems for ensuring that all interviews are well prepared and conducted.

- Every interview should have a clear and specific purpose.

- There should be careful preparation and detailed consideration of lines of questioning.

- Objectives should be tailored to the time available.

- Contentious views on all sides should be tested with equal rigour and uniformity of tone.

- Evasion should be laid bare.

- Interviews should be searching, to the point and always well mannered: they should not be aggressive, hectoring or rude.

- Interviewees must be given a fair chance to respond to questioning.

- Interviewees who make unreasonable demands should be resisted.

- Recorded interviews should be edited fairly.

Generally the guidelines were well received in all quarters. Broadcasters believed this is what they were doing anyway, but it was useful to have it in writing. Politicians felt action had been taken to offer them some protection, and that the BBC was admitting that its house needed putting in order. It is true to say that after their publication interviewers did appear to be more polite; they interrupted less; contentious or complicated questions posed with a demand for a brief answer within the 20 seconds to go before the weather became a rarity; and so too did the out-of-the-blue question about the scandalous activities of a colleague during an interview about traffic congestion.

The BBC has always used 'impartial', 'accurate' and 'objective' as its watchwords in its journalism activities. It is also worth remembering that a person is not obliged to talk to a journalist if they do not want to.

The current guidelines on interviewing vary from those issued internally in 1990, and you can read them in the latest edition of *Producers' Guidelines*, which offers advice and information for anyone involved in the research, production and presentation of programmes or contributions to programmes for broadcast by the BBC. The book is available from the BBC Bookshop and the information is also available on their website.

RULES FOR THE CONDUCT OF INTERVIEWS

The Radio Authority, which licenses and regulates the independent radio industry in accordance with the statutory requirements of the Broadcasting Act 1990, states in its News and Current Affairs Code that licence holders must ensure that:

(a) an interviewee chosen as a representative of an organised group is in a position to speak on behalf of other members or supporters;

(b) where practicable, whether the interview is recorded or live, the interviewee has been made aware of the format, subject matter and purpose of the programme and the way in which his/her contribution is likely to be used;

(c) where practicable, the interviewee has been told the identity and intended role of any other proposed participants in the programme.

On the subject of editing interviews, an extract from the Radio Authority Code of Conduct states that:

> A shortened version of an interview must not misrepresent an interviewee's contribution. An interview should not be edited so as to appear by juxtaposition to associate a contributor with a line of argument which he would probably not accept and on which he is given no opportunity to comment in the programme or feature.

The Code of Conduct also insists that chairpersons, interviewers and phone-in hosts remain impartial. It states:

> A chairman, interviewer or phone-in host should avoid discussion of issues where his connection or involvement away from the programme is such as to call into question his fairness or impartiality. He must ensure that the participant(s) or interviewee(s) – some perhaps with less radio experience than others – are able to express their views; and that the discussion moves forward as coherently and logically as possible. The host, chairman or interviewer must give where appropriate as fair and objective an account as possible of the known opinions of the missing participants on the subject under discussion (NB there are particular requirements under the Representation of the People Act at times of elections). A phone-in host or chairman may assume the position of devil's advocate

to encourage discussion and represent alternative views to those being expressed by his guests (if any) and/or callers. He must not express his own views unless those of opposing views are given the opportunity of expressing them with equivalent force within his programme or the Licence Holder also broadcasts a programme at a similar time of day (in terms of available audience) and of equivalent frequency and duration which features a phone-in host of opposing views.

BROADCASTING STANDARDS

The Broadcasting Standards Commission is the statutory body for standards and fairness in broadcasting. It is the only organisation within the regulatory framework of UK broadcasting to cover all television and radio. This includes the BBC and commercial broadcasters as well as text, cable, satellite and digital services. The Commission has three main tasks, set out in the 1996 Broadcasting Act: to produce codes of practice relating to standards and fairness; to consider and adjudicate on complaints; to monitor, research and report on standards and fairness in broadcasting.

As an independent organisation, the BSC considers the portrayal of violence, sexual conduct and matters of taste and decency in television and radio programmes and advertisements. It also provides redress for people who believe they have been unfairly treated or subjected to an unwarranted infringement of privacy.

Complaints about fairness (unfair or unjust treatment or the unwarranted infringement of privacy) can only be made by those people directly affected by the broadcast, and complaints about standards (violence, sex or issues of taste and decency such as bad language or the treatment of disasters) can be made by anyone who has seen or heard the broadcast.

The majority of complaints received by the Commission are concerned with standards, and as far as radio is concerned these are relatively few compared to the numbers received relating to television broadcasts. Complaints generally include the use of bad or offensive language and sexual innuendo by programme presenters, but occasionally wider issues are raised. The following extract from the BSC bulletin (no. 19, 31 March 1999) illustrates their findings concerning a complaint about an interview broadcast in the James Whale programme on Talk Radio on 24 September 1998 (2200–0100), BSC ref. CN 1229.

The complaint

A listener complained that the Information Officer of the British National Party had been given two hours of airtime in which to defend his party's political views.

The broadcaster's statement

Talk Radio explained that it believed it was very important to distinguish between an interviewee and the interview they contributed. Before the interview, the station had received a number of concerned calls from groups and individuals who felt it should not be providing a platform to an individual who might hold racist views. The station had no desire to provide a platform for doctrinal hatred but believed the right to free speech was too important to give up lightly.

The broadcaster went on to say that the BNP has rightly been accused of racist abuse in its lifetime, and has provoked an angry response as people have sought to restrict its activity. Talk Radio believed that the interview was groundbreaking because it exposed a far greater danger: that the BNP was seeking respectability by attempting to change its image of having a single-issue agenda and was espousing a raft of policies, not just those around immigration, in a manner that seemed entirely reasonable. The interview was conducted as if the BNP were an established party. In so doing, it allowed the party to peel off the thin veneer for itself, exposing how little had changed, but how much more dangerous it had become in its revised presentation. Race was not mentioned for the first half-hour of the interview, and the interview demonstrated that the new image the party was trying to proffer and the subsequent focus on race exposed the superficiality of this change.

The BSC's finding

A Standards Panel listened to the programme. It took the view that the interview had been probing and non-sensational, and considered that the station was justified in reporting in a responsible manner a subject of public interest.

The complaint was not upheld.

To consider and adjudicate on complaints about standards and fairness, the Commission has the power to:

- require recordings of broadcast material (failure to provide a recording is a breach of the Broadcasting Act 1996)

- call for written statements

- hold hearings on the detail of what has been broadcast.

The Commission can also require broadcasters to publish summaries of its decisions either on air or in a newspaper or magazine, and report on any action they might have taken as a result.

All the Commission's decisions are reported in a regular bulletin in printed and on-line versions.

THE ISSUES AND ETHICS OF INTERVIEWING

The regulations that control broadcasters and broadcasting are pretty well laid down and stuck to by radio journalists. Broadcasters and regulatory bodies can offer journalists guidelines that they should follow to keep themselves and the stations out of trouble when conducting interviews. The guidelines are there to lay out the ground rules for those on both sides of the microphone, and because of this you may feel that, working in radio, you don't have to face the same problems as your print colleagues. So how do you feel about the job that you are being asked to do? What is your own personal code of conduct as it applies to interviewing? How do you see the relationship between an interviewer and the interviewee? If you are asked to interview someone you have admired, perhaps a hero or heroine, could you do it without being over-awed or gushing? There will be interview situations that will cause you to stop and think about your role and the effect your involvement in someone's tragedy or triumph plays in their future. There will be occasions when you will worry about whether you are becoming too hardened towards people's grief, and be concerned that you cold-heartedly arrive unannounced on people's doorsteps and intrude on their privacy by asking for an interview at a distressing time. You may be asking questions that your interviewees have never wanted to ask themselves before. There will also be interviews you are asked to conduct that will cause you concern because of your personal beliefs, and raise the question of where you are prepared to draw the line. Can you avoid being judgemental, and ask questions as a devil's advocate? Whatever the subject or whoever the interviewee, remember you are talking to them in your role as a journalist and as such you should act professionally.

As a professional, how far are you prepared to put pressure on a person who says they do not want to be interviewed? Are you prepared to explain to your news editor why you are not prepared to interview someone whose political affiliations appal you? Would you feel the need to express your disapproval of the person you are interviewing? As a vegetarian, could you offer an impartial interview with a local butcher about the benefits of red meat? The radio journalist faces these sorts of dilemma every working day. If you are sent to do an interview you will be expected to come back with something broadcastable and to a tight deadline.

One morning at the newsroom meeting, my editor asked me to go along to a press call being organised by the local police in a town some forty miles away. The police were investigating a fire at a house in which two children had died. They suspected the fire was started deliberately. Despite coverage on radio, TV and in the local newspaper they still had no useful leads. The mother of the dead children had agreed to make an appeal for witnesses, so the local press was invited to hear what she had to say. I was told to come back with something for the lunchtime news. This was to be my first coverage of an 'emotional' appeal.

The press call was attended by a regional TV crew, a handful of reporters and photographers from local newspapers, and me from the local radio station. Accompanied by officers conducting the investigation, the distraught mother was brought before us. The videocam rolled and the camera shutters clicked. An officer introduced the woman and told us she was prepared to answer our questions. There was a long silence. Then one of the journalists asked her 'What is it you want to say?' Through her tears she whispered almost inaudibly 'If anyone knows anything please tell the police.' She then rushed from the room, unable to continue.

The press call was over. The newspaper journalists had enough material to write some copy, the photographers had pictures of the tearful mother, and the TV crew had enough pictures to run along the reporter's voice-over. I felt I had nothing useable in radio terms. The journalists had been seated a distance away so they would appear to be less intimidating. I was inexperienced, and had not thought to place my microphone closer to where the woman would be sitting, so did not get her words on tape. I knew that the best I would be able to give to the editor was a voicer or copy based on what I had seen and heard. I asked the senior officer if he would ask the woman if she would be prepared to record an interview with me in private. I argued that she had obviously felt intimidated by all the journalists present and that the occasion had overwhelmed her, so perhaps she would find it easier to talk one-to-one. I explained that it was not my intention to scoop my colleagues, and that I felt that if any good was to come out of the press call, then a short interview on the radio at lunchtime with the woman speaking in her own words might yield results for the police. The officer was not confident that the woman would agree, as she was very upset, but he said he would ask her. As I waited for him to return I worried that I might have overstepped the mark and could be accused of intruding into the family's grief, but decided that by approaching the woman discreetly via the officer I had acted professionally. If the officer had refused my request out of hand and taken it upon himself not to ask the woman in order to protect her from further upset, I think, as a relatively inexperienced journalist, I would have backed down. Nowadays I would try to persuade him that it was her decision to make, not his.

The woman agreed to be interviewed and I recorded three minutes' worth of material. I was right in my assumption that she had been overwhelmed by the occasion and now agreed to be interviewed because she felt she had let everyone down by her performance at the press call. She also said that she had agreed to talk to me because she was a regular listener to the station, knew my name and had heard other interviews I had conducted, so felt she could trust me to help her get her message across.

The lunchtime news that day carried a wrap featuring my voice report and a clip from the interview. News bulletins for the rest of the afternoon included copy and a clip, the drivetime programme that afternoon included the whole interview, and extracts from the interview were used as part of a package during the following morning's breakfast show. The police reported that they were pleased with the public response to the appeal.

This was a salutary lesson for me and a reminder that I was interviewing real people who were involved in something that would impact on them for the rest of their lives. It was an unexpected experience and I learnt a lot from it. I was very aware that the family, their relatives and friends would probably hear the output generated by that one interview. It was important that nothing broadcast would upset them so I took extra care editing the interview and thought carefully about the words I used in my links and cues. Listening to the original recording of the raw material, I realised that there were a lot of silences that I had not been aware of at the time, but I now appreciate that in sensitive interviewing situations you should not be afraid to stay quiet, and that it is not necessary to fill those pauses with questions or comments, even if the interview is broadcast live. Thinking back on the incident, I feel I was right to press for the interview, but at the same time part of me believes that I only did it because I was afraid of losing face with colleagues in the newsroom and offering the editor next to nothing for a morning's work.

Remember there is no harm in asking more experienced colleagues about how to handle a tricky interview situation. The BBC almost insists on it, as they have a sensible 'refer up' philosophy about anything you may be unsure about. The BBC also publishes its *Producers' Guidelines*, which deals with most of the issues and regulations that face broadcasters, and are based not only on policy decisions but also on the wealth of shared experiences of their staff over the seventy-odd years the Corporation has been involved in broadcasting.

However, sometimes, particularly when you are away from base, you will have to make decisions and take the consequences of your actions. Before that time comes, here is a selection of hypothetical scenarios, based on real situations, that radio journalists may find themselves having to face. Think carefully about how you would handle them. Some of the answers are provided within the book, and some are mentioned in the regulations and guidelines laid down by the broadcasters and regulatory bodies. Try to explain the reason for your decisions.

Scenario 1
You arrive at the scene of a house fire armed with your tape recorder. You interview the fire chief, who tells you that a child died in the fire despite the brave attempt by a neighbour to rescue him from the flames. He points to a man sitting on the garden wall of the house with his face in his hands, and tells you that he is the neighbour. Would you attempt to interview the man? If the answer is yes, how would you approach him and what would you ask? If your answer is no, explain why. Would you

act differently if the man who had tried to rescue the child was the father or close relative?

Scenario 2

You are recording interviews as a member of a team preparing a programme about drugs abuse. One of the researchers tells you that they can arrange an interview with a drug dealer. Do you want to do the interview? The researcher says the dealer has also agreed to let you go along with him to a local pub and, using a hidden microphone, record him doing a deal. Are you up for it? The dealer is asking for a fee for his help and obviously doesn't want his real name used in the introduction to the interview. Is this all OK?

Scenario 3

During the course of recording an interview with a local businessman, he tells you something that he says is off the record. Will you edit it out of the interview before it is broadcast? Can you give reasons for your decision?

Scenario 4

You are working on a consumer programme and there is someone you want to interview about allegations that a former employee has made about his business dealings. For the past ten days you have phoned, faxed, e-mailed and written letters to the former employer requesting an interview with him, but he has so far failed to reply. What can you do to persuade him to record an interview with you?

Someone suggests that you should just turn up at his premises with a tape recorder and ask your questions. Is this a good suggestion?

You decide to doorstep your interviewee and arrive at his premises in time to approach him as he gets out of his car. You switch on your recorder and begin to interview him. Are you within your rights to do this?

The interviewee tells you that he has just returned from a long business trip abroad and will be happy to talk to you if you call him later in the day to make an appointment, because he needs some time to open up his premises and deal with his mail and phone messages, having been away for three weeks. Do you agree?

You arrange an appointment for the next day and put your questions to him. He tells you that the business is no longer his as he sold it during his business trip, and that the former employee who has been making allegations bears him a grudge because he sacked him for passing on business information to a rival company.

What will you do with the interview you have recorded? If you could do the whole exercise again, would you consider doing anything different?

Scenario 5

A politician agrees to be interviewed about a youth project, but on the day of the interview other press have to be kept at bay because they all want his reaction to a controversial news story in the morning papers. The politician agrees to continue with the interview you have arranged provided you do not expect him to comment on the story in the papers. Do you agree? At the interview do you slip in a question about the newspaper story and try to scoop everyone? At the end of the interview do you ask him if he will answer a question about the newspaper story?

Scenario 6

You have just finished interviewing someone who is making headline news and they tell you they have just been paid £500 for an interview with a newspaper and want to know how much they will be paid for your interview? What do you tell them? What will you do if they are unhappy with your reply and say the interview cannot be broadcast until the matter is sorted out?

Scenario 7

You have just completed an interview which was recorded in advance and was based on an embargoed press release which you feel is so revealing that it should be broadcast immediately. Should you ignore the embargo and get your piece on air?

Scenario 8

During the course of an interview, the interviewee becomes distressed and starts to cry. What do you do? Stop the interview and call it a day? Stop the interview until they are able to continue? Leave your tape recorder running? Continue to ask questions?

Scenario 9

Your interviewee has asked to be unnamed on air because they are worried about reprisals for what they will say or because they are embarrassed by their plight. Will this 'remaining anonymous' weaken the authority of the piece or the credibility of the witness?

Your interviewee might be convinced that they will suffer violent reprisals from neighbours, for example. Should you also consider distorting their voice if you are certain the interviewee would suffer if their voice was recognised?

Scenario 10

You have recorded an interview and your interviewee asks you to play it back to her so she can listen to it all. Do you agree? Your interviewee thinks the interview is good and says you must put it out unedited. Do you agree? There is one answer that your interviewee is unhappy about and asks you to cut out. Do you agree? Back at the radio station you get a call from the interviewee asking that another answer she is not happy about be cut out before the interview is broadcast. Do you agree? What if she tells you she got some of the figures wrong and that what she says is incorrect – do you agree to edit it out? Your interviewee calls later to ask if she can hear the edited interview before it is broadcast. Do you agree?

LIBEL

As interviewer you should have at least a basic understanding of the Law of Defamation which covers libel. Even if you do not make a libellous statement, the person you are interviewing may do so. In other words, they may say something during the interview about another person which is regarded by that person as libellous. The alarm bells should start ringing in your head if you hear something which prompts you to ask 'If I were him or her, would I like that said about me?'

- Has your interviewee said something about someone that would cause that person to be shunned or avoided by others?

- Has your interviewee said something about someone that would damage that person's standing professionally or socially?

- Has your interviewee said something about someone that would cause that person to be held up to hatred, ridicule or contempt by others?

- Has your interviewee said something about someone that lowers that person in the eyes of what might be called right-thinking people?

If the answer is yes to any of these questions, then they may have made a libellous statement in the course of the interview and could, along with you and the radio station as publishers of the libel, find themselves in court. The radio station that finds itself in such a position may decide that it has no further use for your services.

The interviewee may not have intended to commit a libel, but ignorance of the law will not help them or you. They may think that because others have been saying the same thing it is all right for them to say it, but they are simply stating a fresh libel to add to the list. They may not have mentioned the person by name, but if it is quite clear who they mean then they have still committed a libel, albeit a nameless one.

If your interviewee has made an inaccurate statement which might cause someone damage, what can you do as an interviewer to avoid broadcasting a libel?

If the interview has been recorded, you should edit out the offending words before transmission of the interview.

If the interview is live and your studio guest makes what you believe to be a libellous statement, then you must distance yourself and the radio station from the statement by offering the speaker the opportunity to withdraw the statement. Use a form of words that leave the speaker and the listener in no doubt that you are distancing yourself from the statement, for example: 'I understand your strength of feeling, but I cannot allow you to say that on air, so will you please withdraw what you have just said?' You should not give them the opportunity to repeat or expand on their statement. Do not involve yourself with the libel by agreeing with the speaker, or by making any noise or comment that would give the impression you are agreeing with the statement or encouraging them to continue with it. Once they have withdrawn their remarks, or if they refuse to withdraw them, you must terminate the conversation with them as soon as possible to avoid any repetition of the statement. By being seen to identify a problem and to distance yourself and the 'publisher', i.e. the radio station, from the statement or comment, you can avoid further trouble.

Members of the public taking part in a phone-in can be unpredictable at the best of times. If a caller makes what you believe to be a libellous statement, you can ask them to withdraw the statement using the words suggested above, or you can simply close the fader on them before they say any more, adding a remark such as: 'I'm going to move on to our next caller before Mr Smith gets himself into trouble by saying any more on that subject.' On independent radio stations there is a delay facility which can used to avoid some problems, and of course most phone-in programme callers are filtered via the programme producer and assistants, who answer the calls and select who goes on air before calling them back and connecting them to the studio.

There are defences to libel if the case should go to court. If the statement made on air is true and evidence can be secured to stand up in court, this is called 'Justification'. If it is claimed that a statement was made in good faith, without malice and in the public interest, this is known as 'Fair comment', provided it is based on fact and again can be proved. The special circumstances in which public interest outweighs an individual's reputation are known as 'Privilege'.

There are other defences, but try not to let it get this far. Efficient preparation, fail-safe routines, secondary-sourcing the information, and thorough research for the interview should establish facts before the broadcast and avoid any nasty surprises on air. Through luck and good judgement, libel cases based on interviews broadcast on radio are rare. The law is complicated and ever changing, so 'if in doubt cut it out', or at least refer to a more senior or experienced broadcaster, or a solicitor. Radio stations are required to keep an audio recording of all their broadcast output as it is transmitted. Among other things, this recording will offer proof of what exactly was said and the action taken by the interviewer on air to diffuse the situation. It is also useful to keep a written log of precautions taken and routines followed by the production team prior to the interview, and in the case of phone-ins a log of the names given by callers, their telephone numbers and the time of the call. This evidence again demonstrates your commitment to avoiding libel.

If you suspect that there are likely to be problems with any interviews that you plan to broadcast, it is a good idea to keep clear records of developments and a diary of how events evolved. Keep a research phone log with dates and times of calls, together with details of who you spoke to and what was discussed. If necessary, advise your superiors and legal advisors at an early stage – even if it all comes to nought, you are covering yourself. Before you confront anyone in an interview situation, you should collect all your corroborated evidence first. Investigate with an open mind and allow for the fact that genuine mistakes are made, and that complaints against someone may be malicious or wrong.

REPRESENTATION OF THE PEOPLE ACT (RPA) 1983

As far as radio broadcasting is concerned, this Act makes sure that coverage of elections is fair, accurate and balanced. Achieving balanced coverage, for example, by inviting all the candidates to take part in a live studio discussion and making sure they all get equal amounts of airtime can be a nightmare. Recording candidates on tape is a safer bet. Keeping a station log of the coverage during an election can help broadcasters to keep tabs on how airtime has been allocated, and acts as a record should there be any queries or disputes after the election. Many stations play it safe and limit their coverage to reports that do not include the candidates.

Most radio stations organise briefings for their staff if an election is in the offing, to make them aware of their responsibilities and the restrictions on them as broadcasters, but it would be worth your while obtaining and reading RPA documents, which tell journalists what they can and cannot cover during the period leading up to an election. Known as the pending period, the duration does vary according to the type of election. If a general election is called, the pending period starts from the time HM the Queen announces the intention to dissolve Parliament through until the polls close on election day. If a by-election is called, the period runs from the date when the writ is issued for the election through until the close of polling. The pending period for local and European elections is five weeks before polling day to the close of polling. If there is a local council election to fill a casual vacancy, the pending period starts from the date when the notice of election is issued.

You are not allowed to broadcast interviews with politicians or those associated with their campaigns during the pending period, unless all the candidates are given equal airtime or waive their right by signing a consent form allowing other candidates to be interviewed. This veto does not apply to coverage of European Union elections. The consent form is usually worded thus:

> Radio X is organising a programme to be broadcast on [date] concerning [constituency/ward] where I am the [party] candidate in the election/by-election to be held on [date].
>
> I understand that under Section 93 of the Representation of the People Act, the consent of all the candidates is required for the broadcast to take place.
>
> I consent to the other candidates taking part in the broadcast without me. I understand the broadcast may be repeated.
>
> I wish/do not wish a statement to be read out on my behalf.
>
> Signed ....   Date ....

PERSONAL SAFETY – GENERAL GUIDELINES

You have a responsibility to look after your own personal safety. Some simple precautions should eventually become second nature.

- Before you go to record your interview on location, make sure someone knows where you will be and when you expect to return. If possible leave a contact name and number and take a mobile phone with you.
- Ensure you have the right clothing for the weather circumstances. Will you need protective or high-visibility clothing?
- Do not use ladders or scaffolding as vantage points.
- Establish the safe escape route in the event of emergency at any premises or site you visit.

If you conduct interviews in a country where the activities of journalists are restricted, you should research further and seek specialist advice. The following advice is based on personal experience and guidelines that Reporters Sans Frontières offers to journalists travelling into a potentially hostile environment:

- Keep those around you informed of your movements.

- If possible go out in groups, and only to places where there are plenty of people.

- Behave in such a way that others will respect you, be reserved with people you meet, and be discreet in your dealings with the public.

- Dress discreetly and never wear clothes that might lead others to be suspicious about your intentions, such as military-style garments.

- Never make a promise of help that you cannot keep.

- Always give the impression that you know where you are and are sure of yourself.

- Try to keep calm if someone is hostile towards you.

Threats of violence

At a Journalism Safety Seminar held at the Freedom Forum on 26 September 1997, BBC Chief News Correspondent Kate Adie said 'the greatest danger I faced in my reporting career was from a saucepan-wielding British housewife'. This from a journalist who has reported from conflicts and war zones all over the world.

Journalists trying to interview those queuing to sign the Princess of Wales Book of Condolence were verbally and physically attacked by members of the public.

You may be interviewing supporters after a football game, demonstrators at a protest march, doorstepping an individual, questioning relatives of a convicted criminal outside a court, or conducting a simple vox-pop. What should you do if someone threatens you with violence?

- Try to appear calm.

- Avoid prolonged eye contact, but do not avoid it altogether. Remove dark glasses.

- Be aware of their tone of voice – it can be an indication to how their attitude may change.

- Speak slowly and softly using simple words and sentences.

- Keep a distance.

- Do not touch the person, or do anything which may be construed as an aggressive act, like pointing a finger or waving a fist.

- Use distraction, try to change the subject.

- Be aware of body language and listen to what they say. Part of the problem may be poor communication and simple misunderstanding.

- Leave the area if you are unable to come to a compromise, or if the situation is getting worse, or if others are starting to join in the discussion. Walk away and out of sight.

INTERVIEWING CRIMINALS

An interviewee becomes the centre of attention for the time they are on air, and what they say and how they behave during an interview can have an impact on the listener. Someone who is normally shunned by a society will often wallow in the media interest shown in them. They will be tempted to boast about and glamorise their activities. You should resist allowing them to do this in an interview. The details of a crime could cause distress to any listener who has been the victim of a similar crime. An impressionable person may be tempted to copy the techniques and commit a similar crime.

A criminal may insist on anonymity – granting it will undermine the authority of your interview.

The police may want to question you about your association with an active criminal.

Is the interview with an active criminal really justified?

Make sure you are aware of the Contempt of Court laws, which are designed to make sure that the course of justice is not perverted, impeded or put at risk of prejudice. Basically, once a criminal case is active, in other words once legal proceedings are under way, then the law comes into force. So if an arrest has been made or a warrant for arrest has been issued, or a person has been charged with a crime either orally or in a written form, then you are restricted and must be careful not to broadcast anything which could be disputed in court.

If, at the end of a case, it is announced that an appeal is to be lodged, the case becomes active again once the appeal is actually lodged. The case is no longer active once it is officially over or if the arrested person is released without charge.

Obviously, the information above does not cover every situation you are likely to come across, so get formal training in the law as it affects journalists in order to avoid the legal minefield.

INTERVIEWING CHILDREN AND INTERVIEWING IN SCHOOLS

A young interviewee should be given the same respect as an older person – this means asking them if they are prepared to be interviewed by you, listening to what they have to say, not talking down to them, and having an honest reason for wanting to use what they have to say. You should prepare for the interview in the same way as you would for any other – research, thinking about possible questions, allowing enough time, etc.

Remember, you must get permission from a parent or guardian before you can interview a child under sixteen years old. If the child is in care and under eighteen years old, you must obtain permission from the local authority. If you are planning to interview children on school premises, you must also get permission from the head teacher.

Experience shows that it can be easier and sometimes more profitable to interview children in groups if you encourage them all to have a say – no more than six at a time and roughly of the same age group.

For best results:

- Allow plenty of time.

- Find a place or room where the children will feel relaxed.

- Sit the children in a circle, in chairs or on the floor.

- Ask any adults present to wait out of the sightline of the children, and not to interrupt or correct anything they say.

- Introduce yourself to the children.

- Demonstrate the portable recorder to them.

- Get them talking about the topic you want to discuss by showing them a relevant picture or artefact, or try playing them sounds on your recorder and asking them to identify what they hear.

- Ask open questions and show an interest in what they tell you.

- Before you end the interview ask them if there is anything else they would like to say.

- Thank them before you leave.

DOORSTEP/AMBUSH INTERVIEWS

For the radio interviewer, this type of interview should be a last resort, and can only be justified when all other approaches for an interview have failed but it is felt that the subject should be asked questions in the public interest. Doorstepping means approaching your interviewee with an open microphone and your recorder running, and asking them questions at the door of their home or place of business. 'Ambushing' refers to attempts to interview someone when they appear in a public place like the street, through their car window etc., without an invitation to do so.

Doorstepping can be seen as an intrusion and could lead to violence, so the interviewer should be clear about what the interview aims to achieve.

If you want to interview someone, the normal procedure is to ask them in advance. You may have justification to doorstep a subject if:

- they fail to respond to repeated requests for an interview via telephone, fax or letter

- they refuse to be interviewed on unreasonable grounds

- they refuse to answer your questions or provide information in another form, e.g. a written statement.

Repeated attempts to secure an interview with someone if you have been refused consent could leave you open to accusations of an unwarranted infringement of privacy.

The Broadcasting Standards Commission Code of Practice (paragraph 25) says:

> People who are currently in the news cannot reasonably object to being questioned and recorded by the media in public places. The questions should be fair even if they are unwelcome. If the approach is made by telephone, the broadcaster should make it clear who is calling and for

what purpose. Nevertheless, even those who are in the news have the right to make no comment or to refuse to appear in a broadcast.

The PressWise Trust, a media ethics watchdog, helps those who feel they have been badly treated by the media, and offers advice to members of the public who find themselves in the news. In its leaflet, 'What can you do when a journalist gets things wrong?', the Trust explains how to deal with unwanted attention:

> If you are approached by journalists for information you are under no obligation to co-operate.
>
> If you would prefer not to get involved, simply tell them, politely but firmly.
>
> Don't be surprised if they persist – that is their job. However, if they refuse to leave your premises or to stop pestering you on the telephone, you are entitled to call the police.
>
> If your refusal to co-operate is used against you unfairly ... you have every right to complain.
>
> If you think a journalist ... or a broadcaster has behaved unethically or unfairly, it is important to complain.

The Metropolitan Police in their 'Note to newsgatherers' advise:

> Newsgatherers should be mindful of the law of trespass. If they are asked by the adult householder, owner or lawful keyholder to leave private premises, they may exacerbate any offence of trespass if they fail to do so immediately.

INTERVIEWING DEMONSTRATORS

Are you attending a demonstration or protest march to collect the views of those taking part in the event, or to report on the behaviour of the demonstrators or counter-demonstrators? If you are honest, it is likely that you set out intending to do the former, and this is what you should hope to come away with on your recorder.

Protests and demonstrations would take place even if the media did not turn up to cover them. However, it is possible that the presence of the media may affect people's behaviour, and so if you feel that actions are being staged to gain your attention then it is probably best for you to withdraw from the scene.

You must not be seen to be directing the event in any way, so when interviewing protesters on a march, walk alongside as you ask your questions, do not ask them to stop or pause.

Try to agree in advance with the organisers where and when you will conduct the interviews. This will help avoid the possibility of trespass by yourself, and should also avoid any unseemly scramble at the end of the demonstration. Make sure you stay on the public side of any barriers erected by the authorities.

CONCEALED RECORDINGS

Recording an interview with someone without their knowledge using a hidden microphone goes against all the guidelines and regulations laid down by regulators, unions and broadcasting organisations, unless it can be shown to be in the public interest. However, it is widely acknowledged that there is a fine line between the public's right to know and an individual's right to privacy.

The BSC Codes of Guidance (paragraph 18) state that:

> The use of secret recording should only be considered where it is necessary to the credibility and authenticity of the story, as the use of hidden recording techniques can be unfair to those recorded as well as infringe their privacy.

You may get permission from your editor to carry out a secret recording if the material is likely to expose a crime, help protect public health or safety, or if it prevents the public from being misled by an individual or organisation. In a press release, Lord Holme, who was appointed Chairman of the Broadcasting Standards Commission on 1 October 1999, said on his first day in office that

> the Commission recognises an overriding public interest can justify both the investigation and broadcast of matters relating to criminal or anti-social behaviour, the exposure of misleading claims or significant incompetence in public office.

Guidelines concerning the recording of interviews by telephone are also very clear:

> Broadcasters should normally identify themselves to telephone interviewees from the outset, or seek agreement from the other party, if they wish to broadcast a recording of a telephone call between the broadcaster and the other party.
>
> (BSC Codes of Guidance, paragraph 22)

4
Advice from the experts

There is no easy route to conducting a successful interview. You need to research the topic and the interviewee, to take control of the interview, to listen to what the interviewee is saying, and to get in plenty of practice. Every interviewer develops their own method and style of working and communicating. The content and style of the interview can also be determined by the programme format, or by editorial considerations that limit and shape how the interview is conducted. Here are a few bits of useful advice from a wide range of practitioners, from both sides of the microphone, on the art of interviewing.

Philippa Dolley is an award-winning reporter working at *Woman's Hour*, and is well known for her ability to handle sensitive subjects and vulnerable interviewees. She spoke to me about the importance of respecting confidentiality and protecting yourself as an interviewer from getting too involved in the story you are telling.

> It is a huge responsibility to interview someone on a subject which is close to their heart. Never force someone to do an interview they are unsure about. It might only be half an hour of your time and five minutes of radio, but they will have to live with the consequences for the rest of their life.
>
> Many people are desperate to have someone to talk to, especially someone without the usual network of friends and family. Because you are taking an interest in them and their story they believe that you genuinely care, and maybe you do, but that is not the reason you are there. As a result they often open up more than they would to any other complete

stranger, and they may say something they later regret. You are in a privileged position and must act with integrity. I always say to people, 'If you think afterwards that you wish you hadn't said something, let me know and I will take it out'. In exceptional circumstances I will play someone the edited version, for example if this is the only way to get them to agree to an interview, but you have to make sure you don't allow them to make your editorial decisions.

Don't underestimate the impact the interview will have on you. I once spent a whole week with a man who was a self-harmer (razor blades mostly). We were retracing his steps and all the places which had treated or mistreated him. By the end of the week I was beginning to think like a self-harmer myself – the build up of tension, knowing you can't resist the act of self-harm, the relief of doing it and the taking care of yourself afterwards. I even started picking at a scab over and over again until it bled. Clearly, I had overidentified and not protected myself from the onslaught of emotion that I was exposed to. In normal circumstances an interview is over within half a day or so, but you can still come away feeling more troubled by their grief than is healthy. This is compounded by the next few days spent editing the interview. My advice is to mentally release the person when you have finished the piece and remember you cannot take on the problems of the world. Just publicising their story is making more people aware.

Brian Jenkins, Head of Radio at the Central Office of Information, offers this advice on building a good working relationship with your interviewee.

The interviewer who impressed me most worked for CBC in Vancouver. She was in London to interview the elderly and ill historian A. J. P. Taylor. As soon as he walked into the room she said to him 'I really love that bow tie you're wearing'. This remark immediately created a comfortable and relaxed atmosphere for the interview. Some interviewers forget that their interviewee is possibly as tense as they are about performing well. It should also be said that if the interviewee is relaxed in the company of an interviewer they may chat away and not realise they have dropped a bombshell, but if they are on their guard they will be especially cautious.

I also think it is important to chat to your interviewee when you are not talking to them on air. For example, I have seen interviewers completely ignore an interviewee during a break for adverts or a piece of music –

when I say ignore I mean not even look at them – and then when the microphone is open again it is all friendly and chatty once more.

Honesty is also important. Recently I recorded an interview with a Minister and it didn't go too well so we tried it again, but the phone rang halfway through the recording. The third attempt was perfect, except that I forgot to switch on the recorder. All you can do in that situation is be up front about it, admit your mistake and hope they will agree to do it again, otherwise you go back to base empty-handed.

Ministers and senior politicians are busy people and always have very full diaries. Time is tight and there is always an aide hovering around trying to keep them moving. If you have arranged an interview, be organised so that recording equipment is set up quickly, the interview carried out efficiently and that you leave immediately you have finished.

Julian Clegg, a Sony Award-winning BBC local radio presenter and journalist with years of experience interviewing personalities, politicians and the public, finds the long-form interview demands that you adopt particular techniques if it is to sound successful.

Generally I find that guests who have come in for a long interview don't like to see the interviewer using pages of notes, after all they won't be using any, and it can give the wrong message that you are not really interested in hearing what they have to say. This applies particularly to guests who are doing the rounds and are being interviewed several times in a week for radio, TV and magazines, and are being asked the same questions over and over again. I would advise committing questions to memory. One way to do this is to divide the interview into chapter headings, and group the areas for questioning into blocks or areas which follow a natural progression.

You need your interviewee to be relaxed, to be at ease with you so that they will tell you things that they wouldn't normally share with a stranger. Try to get them to like you and work at getting on with them. Develop a sort of bedside manner and listen to what they are saying. Their attitude to you may be influenced by the location of the interview. If it is in the studio they can be distracted by all the equipment and activity, but they will feel more in control of the proceedings if you are on neutral ground like their hotel suite.

In the long-form interview you do not want your interviewee to deliver what you want from them straight away; the interview should develop and gradually reveal information. You should do as little talking as possible and let your interviewee take over for parts of the interview. The danger point is when you move on from their reason for taking part in the interview, say to plug their new book, show, etc., and start to talk about areas that interest you, but which they may be wary of discussing or having delved into.

Helen Lloyd is Oral History Producer at Radio WM and BBC Coventry & Warwickshire, and has had plenty of experience of interviewing for montages. Follow her advice if you are planning to cut out your questions.

When you are interviewing for montage features, the wording of your questions does not have to be as precise as when you are interviewing for other sorts of programme. If you know you are going to cut out your voice, then you can be as woolly as you like and this often gets better answers, because the interviewee feels under less pressure, and is encouraged to use a more relaxed and conversational tone.

If you know that you will need the answers to your questions to stand alone for a montage, and want to lead into them without including your own voice asking the question, then get your interviewee to introduce the answer for you. For example if you ask 'What effect did the war have on your career plans?', and she replies 'Oh, it was a major blow to them', then ask her to 'make sense of that' by including the question in her answer 'The war was a major blow to my career plans.' This technique is particularly useful if you are interviewing for unlinked montages when much of the material needs to be juxtaposed.

There can be problems, because some people find this concept harder to grasp than others who have no difficulty with it. I have to say that this ability to grasp it or not has nothing to do with the age or intelligence of the interviewee. So if the technique isn't working you have to stop using it. Then you have to just hope for the best and concentrate on listening out for bits of the interview that will stand alone.

The technique can also be disruptive to the interviewing process because you are having to interrupt the interviewee. Obviously you have to be extra careful if they are talking about a deeply emotional subject. You can't interrupt them, so you have to keep a lot in your head until the time is right.

Usually when you are interviewing to a tight news deadline and working within a journalist's agenda, you have to stay focused on the story, avoid going off at tangents, and listen out for clues that something interesting has been said that you can clip out for your piece. Collecting material using oral history techniques can be liberating. If you give the interviewee some element of control by allowing them the time and freedom to go off at a tangent, you can be suprised by some of the things they talk about. Those of us working on *The Century Speaks* felt we had recorded some of our best-ever interviews this way.

Natalie Graham, Bi-Media Broadcast Journalist BBC South, explains how to cope with juggling the demands of interviewing someone for both TV and radio at the same time.

The bi-media journalist is expected to collect interview material for both television and radio. Inevitably the radio material suffers, because deadlines mean you have to cut corners and the interviewee does not have the inclination to be put through an interview twice on the same subject. This means you end up just using the TV audio as your radio interview, and they are not well matched because the interviewing technique is different. Quite often priorities mean that you have to concentrate on processing the TV material so you end up just feeding raw unedited audio to the radio producer. If you try to produce both a TV and a radio package you end up working a fifteen-hour day.

I always try to tell the interviewee what I'm doing and explain how I am going to do it. This helps them to cope with any instructions I may need to give them like 'can you run that sentence in with that sentence then I will have a nice clip that I can use'. It sounds silly, but when you are interviewing a head-to-head for radio it is important to remember to make sure your voice is also on mike, which we often don't bother with on TV because the question will more than likely be edited out anyway. You also have to remember to record a proper interview for the radio, one that flows and makes sense, rather than interviewing with random questions that will elicit answers for clips.

Russell Fuller, sports reporter for BBC 5 Live, has this to say about interviewing sportspeople:

I'm not sure if the technique of interviewing is that different for sport. It can be very difficult to get a decent response when a match has just finished, because the interviewee is exhausted, emotional or desperate for a shower, and is not in a very good position to give a considered view on the match they've just taken part in. They tend to go onto auto-pilot and keep talking without actually saying anything.

I suppose the key is to ask a question they are not really expecting, which might make them stop and think about the reply instead of just repeating what they say after every other game.

If you are conducting more considered interviews, then it is important to be well prepared, because football managers, like some politicians, will not suffer fools gladly.

Personal contacts are a major help, particularly when you are looking for an interview in a huge media scrum.

If there is time I often ask a couple of general questions first, which I probably will not use, just to warm up the interviewee.

Sue Littlemore, BBC Education Correspondent, offers the following advice for correspondents:

The three watchwords of a correspondent should be distil, distil and distil. You will not win any awards for purple prose, so keep whatever you are going to say simple, keep to the nub of the story and do not go down any other avenue, and be wary of quoting lots of figures and statistics. This can be the most difficult thing in the world if you are being interviewed about a complicated subject, but it's easy to confuse yourself and the listener. The listener only has one chance to take in what you are telling them.

To avoid getting into a muddle, think about what you are going to say and what you want to say before you go on air.

Often there is no time available to have a discussion with the interviewer/presenter before going on air; they may be already broadcasting live. I may not even know if they have been fully briefed about the interview, or if they have been provided with any questions. I usually do not have advance notice of the questions I will be asked, but what I try to do is make sure that whatever the question I will get in the bit that I had planned to say. It sounds difficult, and it is, but it is all a matter of practice and experience.

Chris Todd is a regular interviewee on radio, usually talking about environment issues. What qualities does he think are required to make a good interviewer?

> I like an interviewer who understands the topic we are discussing and who does not waste air-time going over old ground. I want to use the time to put my message across, which is the reason why I have been asked on to the radio, and what I think the audience wants to hear. I always know if the interviewer is listening to the answers I am giving because they will ask follow-up questions and begin to probe the subject and challenge my answers, which I think makes for a more interesting listen.

> I prefer face-to-face interviews, but if the interviewer goes over the top with encouragement by nodding too much I find it can be a distraction. On the other hand, a down-the-line interview from an empty, unmanned studio where you are talking to a blank wall, getting feedback and the like down the headphones and possibly getting cut off mid-interview, is worse.

Louisa Brooke, a radio researcher working for *The World Tonight* on BBC Radio 4, regularly finds and talks to potential guests on the telephone.

> Oh, the joys of phone-bashing. I've gradually got over my fear of doing it. When I first started researching I was working with one other producer in a tiny office, and I actually sent him to the canteen for coffee when I first started phone-bashing because I felt so self-conscious in front of a more experienced journalist.

> My best tips? Sounds stupid, but being friendly does matter – especially if you are talking to people who you are likely to use again. Keep track of the people you talk to, because a good contacts book is essential. Don't be afraid to ring up people for their advice. If you have a wide brief you may not know who the best people are to speak to, but pressure groups and other journos, etc., can often point you in the right direction. If in doubt put out as many feelers as possible. Don't just rely on a couple of people – talk to as many as you can. You can always turn down interviewees if you find someone better, but if you don't have any interviewees in the first place ...

> Be flexible in your approach, depending on who you are talking to. Professionals like press officers deal with enquiries all the time and are

worth having on your side, but with non-professionals like the public you need to make sure you allay any fears they have about the press by being very clear about what it is you want. Sometimes it is useful to be friendly and funny, other times to be completely professional. Remember that the people at the other end of the phone are just that, people, and usually don't bite.

Donna Alos recently graduated from a journalism degree course and is now Senior Journalist at South City FM. She remembers her first attempts at interviewing:

I found some people were very defensive when they were approached for an interview for radio, and I was put off by their brash and sometimes aggressive attitude towards me. I found that the best way to cope with it was to be polite to them and smile a lot. I also watch my body language and make sure I give them as much encouragement to talk as possible, for example by nodding and looking sympathetic. My main concern, however, was that I wouldn't be able to get the equipment to work and would end up without an interview and looking stupid in front of the interviewee. When I was conducting interviews I quickly realised that you should not be afraid to ask basic questions, especially if it is a subject you or your listener perhaps knows very little about. I used to be scared about having to interview someone, but not now. It does get easier as time goes by.

Fran Acheson, Chief Instructor (Production) at BBC Radio Training, and a documentary producer, has this to say:

If you are going off to interview someone about events that may have happened some years ago, you should take along some pictures from magazines or newspapers showing coverage to help remind your interviewee and stimulate their responses. Another good tip to stimulate memory, and therefore revelation, is to encourage an interviewee to bring out their photograph album if they have any relevant pictures of people or places involved in the story.

Paul Rowinski, investigative reporter and lecturer, offers up these insights:

In the early stages of an investigation when you are trying to get a source to name names, interviews are often clandestine because the source is afraid of being exposed as a whistle blower. A lot of time has to be spent edging around the subject of your interview just to firm up facts, to substantiate and confirm information, and to cross-check the agenda of your source. Interviewing may have to be off the record at this stage because you are talking to a source who wants to talk, but may have to be convinced that he wants to talk. To avoid abuse, any request for anonymity should be considered in the context of the gravity of the information that is being provided.

When you eventually confront someone with allegations, it is important that you do not cut to the chase too soon – ask them plenty of open questions and allow them to put across their version of events. Do not be afraid to conduct the interview at a slow pace, and don't jump in with another question straight away at the end of a reply because hopefully the interviewee will feel obliged to fill the silence with more information. Allow your interviewee to fill in gaps in your knowledge by asking for clarification of facts and rumours, then hopefully the stage will be set for them to fall on their own sword.

In radio there are time constraints, but if you want the interview to be good radio by building up anticipation, then it is probably a good idea to save the best question until last, rather than cutting to the chase and confronting the interviewee at the start.

5
Technical advice

After years of stability, the equipment used in radio broadcasting has started to develop and change more often. The move away from analogue equipment, which has been the basis of recording and editing techniques, is due to the introduction of digital technology. The result is better quality recordings, lighter and more compact equipment, and the introduction of computer technology to editing and studio facilities.

Following Thomas Edison's pioneering work and inventions which enabled him to record sound, subsequent developments in tape-recording equipment contributed to the techniques and acceptance of using recorded material for broadcasting, and offered variety and flexibility to broadcasters and programme makers. From the use of the 'recording vans' in the 1930s, which were used to record location sound onto wax discs, through to the heavyweight 'Midget' portable tape recorders of the 1940s, radio reporters and correspondents on location, whether in the hop fields of Kent or the battlefields of France, were able to at last collect and store material which could be edited, with some difficulty, before being broadcast. Studios once resembled the engine room of an ocean-going liner, equipped with huge tape recorders and mixing desks and a bewildering array of lights and switches that would baffle a pilot of Concorde. Today's studios have a minimalist feel and boast touch-screen facilities. The technology may have developed, the quality of recordings improved and the equipment may be lighter and easier to use, but the basic principles of how the interview is collected have stayed more or less unchanged.

OPERATING PORTABLE EQUIPMENT

The portable tape recorder or its disk equivalent is in effect the radio journalist's notebook or the photojournalist's camera, and goes everywhere they go. These machines differ from the ones often used by print journalists. The 'memo'-type models that are used as *aides-mémoire* often rely on built-in microphones and will not produce broadcast-quality recordings, and if the machine fails then the journalist can always rely on pen and paper to record what was said.

As a radio interviewer, if your tape recorder fails when you are recording an interview you will have nothing to broadcast, so do everything possible to avoid this situation arising.

You should be able to demonstrate practically and verbally your skill in handling portable audio equipment in a manner that is safe, competent and does not damage the equipment. Once the equipment has been demonstrated to you, or you have carefully read the operating instructions that came with it, then work through the following self-assessment before you try to carry out any interviews.

- Equipment – Do I know what equipment makes up the kit (including microphone, batteries, mains lead, headphones, etc.)? Am I familiar with the appropriate terms? Do I know how it should be transported and stored?

- Assembly – Can I assemble/disassemble the kit in a logical order (this saves time and avoids errors being made)? Once assembled, do I know what it can do? Can I check it functions correctly?

- Handling – Can I operate it correctly? Can I operate it in different positions and locations?

- Basic troubleshooting – Can I find, identify and rectify simple faults? Can I identify faults that require a technician's assistance?

Once you are confident you can operate the equipment, it's time to dip your toe into the water and start using it. Before you start any recording you should first 'take level', to ensure that the recording is at the correct level to avoid any distortion. It is very important that you get a good quality recording. If you record at too high a level the sound may distort and be unusable. If you record at too low a level you may be able to boost the level in the studio, but the poor quality of the recording will still be noticeable, particularly if you are using tape, as the background hiss that you get on all recordings will also be amplified.

Practise taking level with a variety of tape recorders and microphones. Some portable recorders have an ALC (Automatic Level Control) or ARL switch (Automatic Record Level) which, as the name suggests, will keep your input signal at a set level by continually adjusting it without you having to monitor it during a recording. However, there are disadvantages in that you will get variable levels because the machine cannot distinguish between sounds and always listens out for the loudest. So if you are recording an interview in the street with traffic noise in the background and your interviewee pauses, the machine will then bring up the sound of the traffic because it is attempting to compensate for what it senses to be a drop in level. Then when your interviewee speaks again it rushes to keep the level down. So why bother to use it? There will be occasions when you are trying to concentrate on your interviewee and cannot afford to keep looking away to check levels. For example, I used this facility when I was recording an interview aboard a lifeboat in the English Channel and having to be sick over the side at the same time. Operating the levels manually will give you more flexibility and control over your recording.

So how do we take level on a portable tape or disk recorder?

- Plug the microphone into the recorder.

- Load a tape or disk.

- Put the recorder into record and pause mode.

- Speak into the microphone. Watch the level meter and adjust the record input accordingly.

Try the following exercises at work or at home. The first exercise is designed to get you used to operating the recorder and raising your awareness of the acoustics around you; the second will get you used to hearing your own voice; and the third puts you on the first rungs of experiencing what it is like to conduct an interview.

Exercises

Switch on your recorder and leave it running in the record mode, plug in the microphone and go on a walkabout around the building into the different spaces that it
offers, recording the sounds as you go. Hold the microphone slightly in front of you or
by your side and walk through the office, head down the stairs, make a quick visit to
the loo, travel down in the lift, walk through the canteen, into the car park, head back
through reception, along the corridor, pop into the studio, spend half a minute in a
cupboard (make sure someone is around to let you out), then go up the stairs back to
the office. Now play back the tape or disk and listen to the different acoustics and
noises you have recorded. Listen out for the characteristics that make up the acoustics
of each individual room or area. Note which sounds dominate and illustrate a particular environment, those which are in the background, and those sounds you were not
aware of when you walked through a space.

Now do the exercise again and try to record yourself giving a running commentary as
you go walkabout. When you play back, listen to the balance between your voice and
the background sounds, and the way the voice sounds in each different acoustic.
Compare how your voice sounds in the loo to how it sounds in the studio or cupboard.

Take your recorder and microphone out into the street, to the park or into the garden.
Find somewhere to sit where you can get a good view around you. Switch on the
recorder, take level on your voice, and then spend two minutes carefully describing the
scene around you as though you were describing it to a person who cannot see. Keep
your recording continuous, do not use the pause button to stop the tape running, but
don't be afraid to pause occasionally and let the natural sounds fill the gaps. You may
have the microphone too close to your mouth or too far away, or you may dry up and
not be able to think of what to say, so you might need to try this exercise a few times
before you are happy with the results. Before you start speaking, decide how you are
going to describe the scene. Try describing the view from left to right, or start with a
distant view and gradually move closer to where you are sitting. You have to think
rather like a film director working with long shots, close-ups and panning shots. The
combinations and variations are endless, so don't rush this exercise. Play back the
results to a friend when you get back to base and see if it conjures up a picture in their
mind. Don't record more than two minutes, otherwise it may have the same effect on
them as showing those endless holiday snaps.

Now you feel a bit more confident about handling the portable recorder, you are more aware of the nature of sound, and you feel a little happier about hearing your own voice coming out of the speaker or headphones. So now is the time to tackle your first interview. Put in a call to 10 Downing Street and arrange an appointment with the PM. Better still, ask a friend or relative if they are prepared to let you ask them half-a-dozen questions on a set topic in the comfort of their own home. Once you have agreed a subject ('childhood memories', 'looking after tropical fish', 'my favourite place', etc.), jot down a few questions to get you started (Where is your favourite place? Why do you like it there? What do you do when you go there?). Once the interview is in full swing, questions should arise naturally out of the answers you are being given. Remember to switch on your recorder and take level on both your voices before you start the interview. When you have finished recording, play back the interview and listen to it. Are the levels of the two voices about equal or is one louder than the other? Was there any microphone rattle? Did the interview follow a logical order? Which bits would you edit out? What is the duration of the interview – longer or shorter than you imagined?

Now do the interview again, but choose a different topic to interview your friend about, and move to a different location like the kitchen, the garden or the street, to hear the effect that the acoustics and the background noise have on the recording.

Remember that after using your portable recorder you should recharge the batteries if the equipment is designed to allow you to do this. Your machine will then be ready at a moment's notice. Whenever possible, use your portable recorder as a mains-operated machine; if you are recording an interview indoors, take along a mains lead so that you can operate off mains power and save battery power.

CHOOSING A RECORDER

There are a number of different types of recorders: open-reel, cassette, DAT and minidisk.

Open-reel machines use spools of recording tape. Portable models you may come across are Uher and Nagra. They come in mono and stereo models, and despite being analogue and very heavy to carry are still used professionally. The Uher has been a firm favourite with BBC interviewers for many years, but is gradually being replaced by digital lightweight recorders. BBC staff who use Uhers on a regular basis have often suffered from a complaint affectionately known as 'Uher shoulder'. For studio use you find the range includes Revox, Tascam and Studer.

Cassette recorders use standard cassettes. Portable models favoured by radio stations include Marantz and Sony Pro. Cassette recorders have been used widely in commercial radio for a number of years; interviewers preferred them to the bulky Uher.

DAT recorders come in portable and studio models, and use a digital cassette which is smaller than standard cassettes but is bigger than those you find in dictating- or memo recorders. Sony DAT recorders are widely used by BBC producers, and are replacing Uhers as the favoured portable machine.

Minidisk recorders are becoming increasingly popular in both portable and studio models. Professional models are not available so the industry is using domestic models. They are lightweight, easy to use and cheap to replace. Because they are designed for domestic use they are prone to damage through overuse and transporting, so they can be bought ready mounted in a specially designed carry case. The case is fitted with rechargeable batteries and heavy duty connectors. Microphone connectors on the minidisk are susceptible to damage. The case makes the interviewer look more professional, and many interviewers say the hand-held standard minidisk appears less threatening to a nervous interviewee and is less visible a temptation to would-be thieves.

TAPE, CASSETTES AND DISKS

Open-reel tape comes on 13cm (5in), 18cm (7in) and 26.5cm (10in) plastic spools, which at a recording speed of 19cm (7.5in)/sec will store 15, 30 and 60 minutes of material.

Cassettes are available in durations of about ten minutes to 120 minutes. But the recommended tape should be no longer than a C60 (thirty minutes per side). Longer tape tends to be thinner and more likely to get damaged in the machine. Remember to wind the cassette on a short way past the protective leader tape at the start before you begin recording, or you may lose the opening words of your interview.

DAT tapes and minidisks record and play on one side only, so do not try to turn the cassette over when you reach the end.

In some studios you will also come across tape cartridges which are used to play out short pieces of audio. Other studios favour the use of computer discs for this purpose.

Only recordings made onto open-reel tape can be edited directly. If your recording is on cassette, DAT, minidisk, etc., it will need to be dubbed or copied onto open-reel tape, or downloaded into a computer, to enable editing to proceed.

CHOOSING AND USING MICROPHONES

The microphone is the ear of the recorder. It picks up sounds in the air. However, unlike the human ear, which is connected to the brain, a microphone cannot be selective about the sounds it hears. If you are talking to someone in a crowded room you will probably not have much difficulty in hearing and understanding what they say to you. A microphone, on the other hand, cannot focus on the individual voice and isolate it, but will pick up the overall sound of the room.

More often than not your tape recorder will come with a general purpose microphone which should cope with general recording situations. All microphones sound different, and you may find one sort works better than another, depending on what you want it to do. Experiment with your microphone and get to understand its limitations. The important consideration is the 'polar diagram', that is the pattern of the area and direction of the sound that the microphone is able to pick up.

The most common microphone used for location recordings of radio interviews and studio interviews is known as 'cardioid'. This sort of microphone picks up sounds coming from one direction; that is the area directly in front and to the side of the microphone. Imagine a heart-shaped pattern around the tip of the microphone (hence the name cardioid). Because the microphone does not pick up the sounds at the cable end it is important that it is pointed in the direction of the sound source, otherwise the sounds or voices will sound 'off mike'. Cardioid microphones can be hand-held on location and attached to a microphone stand for studio use.

A 'figure of eight' microphone is shaped differently to a standard cylindrical microphone; it is squatter and flatter and will pick up sounds from two directions, the front and the back. This is why it is favoured for one-to-one interviews or double-headed presentation across the table in a studio. It is usually mounted in the centre of a studio table. The shape and weight of the figure of eight makes it awkward to be hand-held.

The 'omnidirectional' sort of microphone will pick up sounds equally all round, it so is useful for round-table discussions, picking up audience reactions, or location recording when the sound mix demands more than the focused recordings a cardioid microphone will produce. The microphone looks similar in shape to the cardioid and can also be hand-held and attached to a stand for studio use.

Something else you will need to check is how the microphone is powered. If it uses a battery then always carry a spare, remember to switch it on and off, and check it is working before you start your interview.

All microphones have a small windshield attached to them, but sometimes extra protection may be needed against 'popping' if you or your contributor is too close to the microphone, and for recording in blustery conditions on location. These windshields or pop-shields are made of a foam-like material and slip over the top of the microphone without reducing the sound input level unless they become rain-soaked.

Sometimes using a hand-held microphone can be inconvenient for the interviewer, or intrusive and even threatening to the interviewee. Small cardioid microphones that attach to the clothing with a clip can be a useful alternative. Known as lapel, tie-clip or clip microphones, they are lightweight and are soon forgotten by the wearer. They should be attached to the chest area of the interviewee, and are capable of picking up the voice even though your contributor will be speaking towards you rather than angling their head to speak downwards into the microphone. The interviewer can also wear one, and if your recorder is a stereo model both microphones can be plugged into it.

THE RADIO CAR

The radio car is provided with a talkback facility which enables the person on location to communicate off air with a studio or newsroom back at base. When they arrive on site they can call up the studio and ask for the signal quality and level from the radio car to be checked prior to transmission. Once the mast is functioning and the microphone operational, the base studio can feed the station output into the headphones of the interviewer or reporter at the car. They can then pick up from presenter or newsreader and make their live contribution into the station's output. The car should also have headphones for reporter and interviewee, and input sockets which allow the playing of taped interviews into a live programme.

You will need full training in how the car functions and the safety aspects of its use before you can hit the road. You will probably be expected also to take a short driving test.

REMOTE STUDIOS

Remember to arrange access and for the power to be switched on, as the studio is usually unmanned.

The advantage of the system is that you get a good quality signal both ways on a dedicated line to and from the base studio.

Initial contact with the interviewee to establish the line is made via the telephone, but is then switched and the microphone and headphones replace the telephone. The interviewee will have to open up microphone faders on the mixing desk. Remind your contributor to switch off the power at the end of the interview.

A sheet with straightforward operating instructions should be available on the studio desk. A copy should also be available at the station base in case there are any queries.

PHONES AND LANDLINES

In the studio, when using phone contributors, make sure they position their mouth close enough to the handset to give a clear signal, but not too close or with too loud a voice as to distort – the same procedure for a guest in front of a microphone. Check they can hear the output of the station, not just the studio, if you are going to interview them live into a programme.

The station will be equipped with a telephone balance unit, like a small switchboard, which allows the telephone contribution to be switched to the mixing desk and put to air by opening the appropriate fader.

The reason why telephone lines sound crackly is because they are being used by a number of callers at the same time, but it is possible to rent a dedicated line which is used by the studio and the contributor for the duration of the interview. The resulting call will be close to studio quality.

RADIO STATION STUDIOS

Walk around your home and spend a minute or so in each room with your eyes closed. Listen to the sound of the room. If you clap your hands or speak loudly you will hear the sound bounce off the walls, floor and other hard surfaces of the bathroom, and be aware of the 'bright' or 'live' sound of the space; but in the room with the sofa, armchairs, carpet and curtains, you will notice how the sound does not come back at you quite so sharply. The 'indirect' sounds are absorbed by the furnishings and the room sounds 'dead'.

Radio station studios are designed to sound 'dead', that is to absorb as much as possible the indirect sound that bounces around the room, so that the microphones only have to deal with the direct sound of the voice speaking into them. That is why you will see acoustic boxes and tiles on the ceiling and walls and carpets on the floor. The aim is to produce good quality, clear 'direct' sound for the listener.

Back in your home, try listening with your eyes closed to the sounds in one of the rooms. You will hear traffic noise coming from the street and children playing in the garden. The longer you listen you will become aware of other sounds, like the central heating radiators, the strip light's buzzing or the refrigerator humming. The room is not as quiet as you first thought. The studios at a radio station are also insulated as well as treated for sound. The walls contain thick insulation, the windows are double-glazed and sealed, and the double doors will be specially lined – this is why they are so heavy – to prevent extraneous sound entering the studio.

When the microphones are 'live', that is to say in use, a red warning light is automatically switched on to warn anyone outside the studio to remain outside the studio.

The studio/control room will usually contain a mixing desk into which equipment is linked. This equipment provides sound sources and includes microphones for the programme presenter or the interviewer, microphones for the interviewee, open-reel tape recorders, cart or dart machines, DAT and cassette recorders and CD and minidisk recorders and computers, which are used for recording, editing, storing and playing audio material.

Studios are often organised so that they can be self-op (self-operated) which means that if you are conducting a live or recorded interview you will also have to operate the mixing desk faders, set up microphones, operate the recording equipment and check the levels of the recording as the interview proceeds.

Another studio may contain a round table covered in acoustic material, on which will be placed about three microphones and headphones: this is used for live and recorded interviews and 'round table' discussions. The microphone levels will be operated by someone seated at the mixing desk in an adjoining control room. The interviewer and guests sit at the table. The interviewer wears headphones so that they can hear any messages via the talkback system linked to the control room. Producers who need to speak to the interviewer via their headphones should follow these directions:

- Check and adjust the interviewer's headphone volume.

- If the guests are wearing headphones, make sure they will not hear your messages to the interviewer.

- Speak to the interviewer at normal volume – no shouting or whispering into their ear.

- Remember that the interviewer will be trying to listen to the interviewees, so only speak when it is absolutely necessary. Pre-interview preparation and discussion should sort out the logistics of the interview.

- Keep anything you say short and to the point.

- Try not to speak to the interviewer when they are speaking themselves; all but the very experienced will probably stumble over what they are saying. No particular time is ideal, but it is best to wait until the guest is answering the question.

THE BULK ERASER

This piece of equipment is used to 'clean' audio tape of material that has been recorded onto it. It works by generating a magnetic field that scrambles the recording. When using the bulk eraser, keep your watch or tapes that you do not want cleaned away from the equipment.

NEWSROOM AND PRODUCTION OFFICE

Newsrooms come in all shapes and sizes, but at most stations now an open-plan office will be shared by programme production teams or individuals and the news team. They will all have access to telephones and a computer. There will also be a newsfeed, audio and text editing facilities, and storage systems. Equipment may also be available to enable interviewers to conduct and record phone interviews at their desk.

SAFETY PRECAUTIONS

- Always lock away any equipment in the boot of the car when on location.

- Unplug any electrical equipment that comes into contact with liquids and have it checked before using it again.

- Make sure you know how to cope with a victim of electric shock and also how to avoid becoming a victim yourself.

- Do not expose any equipment or recordings to heat, cold, moisture, dust or direct sunlight.

- Store recordings carefully:

  - Keep them away from magnetic fields.

  - Keep tapes in their boxes, and with open-reel tape store with tail out to avoid problems with print-through and adhesion.

  - Stack open-reel tapes flat – if they are kept on their side for a long period then the effects of gravity will cause side pressure to mis-shape the tape, leading to distortion and adhesion problems during playback.

To prevent recordings on cassettes from being erased or recorded over, remove the safety tabs at the rear of the cassette using a small screwdriver or similar device. Should you decide to use the cassette for another recording, you can cover the holes with sticky tape to allow this.

6

Before the interview

SOURCES OF STORIES

Ideas for interview material can come from a range of sources. There will be press or news releases from pressure groups, charities, central and local government departments, etc. Copies of agendas and minutes of meetings will be sent to you. Surfing the internet will give you ideas; so too will conversations you overhear in pubs and on buses. News services and news agencies will supply information. You will get calls from, or make check calls to, emergency services; you will receive tip-offs from colleagues and even listeners to the radio station. Articles and interviews in newspapers and magazines will give you ideas which you can approach from a different angle or develop into a follow-up. Your own local knowledge or specialist interest will be invaluable when hunting out potential subject-matter and contacts.

In order to conduct an interview you need to approach the source of the story to find someone to talk to you, but remember not everything you will be told will be worth following up.

You may also need to check the information with another source to confirm that the facts are correct. You should be critical in your choice of source, and the authority of your source should be carefully evaluated.

PRESS RELEASES

Every day, news editors, programme editors, programme producers and presenters receive a large number of press releases through the post or via fax or e-mail from organisations, groups and businesses all trying to 'make the news'. Some of this mail will be put straight into the waste bin because it is simply promotional or advertising material; some will be filed away to be looked at again a day or so before the event being publicised.

Press or news releases come in all shapes and sizes. Some will be a few lines long, while others will contain extracts from speeches or publications. Some are pure propaganda, or offer specific reaction to a current news story, or make an official statement about an issue.

Organisations such as councils, committees, charities, companies, pressure and action groups, the police, etc., issue press releases in the hope of attracting the attention of the press and media, who will then pass on the information to their listeners, viewers and readers. Press releases are also sent to inform the media about a press conference or launch. Press releases often contain quotes from a spokesperson, which is fine if you are a print journalist, but you may need to remind the press officer who wrote the release that for radio you will need to record an interview, maybe just on the phone, with someone. What you do not want is for the spokesperson to simply read their quote verbatim from the press release. When an organisation issues a press release, report or statement, it may offer someone up for an interview from a studio via IRN or a BBC newsroom, or via a telephone or ISDN line so that individual stations can arrange to conduct a two-way using their own local interviewer. The station simply has to contact the designated representative at the organisation and arrange a time and duration for the interview.

Some press releases are embargoed, which means the information cannot be broadcast or published until after a specific date and time. Embargoes are usually respected. This does not mean you cannot start preparing the story for broadcast. For example, you may want to arrange an interview with someone mentioned in the release and record it as soon as possible, so that when the embargo is over you will have your interview, package, wrap or feature ready to go on air. Do bear in mind that the situation or details could change before the story goes out on air; your interviewee may have even been replaced in post and no longer have the authority to speak to the press; or the press office may send out further updated facts and figures in a follow-up release. If you break an embargo applicable to a government or parliamentary document you run the risk of being in breach of parliamentary privilege.

When deciding whether to follow up the contents of a press release you should think about why it was released. You will have to decide who you think will gain from any information that you broadcast. Press releases are not broadcast verbatim, but the information within them can be used as the starting point for setting up a news story, an interview or even an entire programme.

HOW DO WE DECIDE ON THE FOCUS OF THE STORY?

Time is tight on radio in the same way that space is limited in print. You cannot afford to put a rambling, unfocused interview on air. If the focus or angle of the interview is not obvious, then take the following into account:

- Will the subject under discussion or the identity of the interviewee be of interest to your audience – the listeners to the station on which the interview will be heard?

- Does the interview cover any topics that will be of particular interest to listeners in a specific local area or those with a specialist interest, or is it of general human interest?

- Is the interview about a topical subject, or is it with someone who is currently newsworthy?

- Will the interview reveal new information, explain the reasons for conflict or disagreement, or summarise an ongoing situation?

- How much time is the interview worth, given the restrictions on airtime within a bulletin or programme?

PLANNING THE INTERVIEW

Before you get to the stage of recording or broadcasting an interview, you can make the process easier by careful planning and research. If you do not research effectively, are unsure of your facts, or are not aware of the other side of an argument, how can you challenge your interviewee's views?

As part of your planning for the interview, try to pre-hear the finished product – this may make it easier to prepare and conduct the interview. This technique can also help keep you focused on the subject of the interview throughout the process.

The three ingredients you need to consider are preparation, organisation and communication.

Preparation

- What is the audience profile of the station that will broadcast the interview?

- Why have I chosen this person to interview?

- What is the subject of this interview?

- How does the interview fit into the programme or bulletin?

- Why do I want to ask them these questions?

- Who are the alternative interviewees?

- What do I need to know about the subject of the interview?

- What do I need to know about the interviewee?

Organisation

- Will the interview be more effective live or recorded in the studio or on location?

- Do I need to book equipment, studios, transport, staff, etc.?

- What needs to be done to ensure the best use is made of any location sounds?

- Should I have a list of alternative interviewees – and an alternative focus for the piece if it needs to change?

Communication

- Discuss the interview with the interviewee in broad terms. Are you prepared to cancel or change tack if new information comes to light?

- Listen and watch the way the interviewee communicates – it will help in the planning of the interview. You may decide the interviewee would be better for a pre-recorded interview rather than a live appearance.

- Don't grill the interviewee too much during your initial contact.

You need just enough information to get an idea of what they will or won't say.

- Give the interviewee the opportunity to correct any major inaccuracies in your research notes.

- Make sure that the interviewee is clear about what you need, and check if there is anything more they need to know.

- Make sure everyone involved is clear about when and where it will be happening.

TIME MANAGEMENT

Whenever you do any job or task for the first few times, you wonder whether you are spending too much time on it. How many interviews should you be able to fix and research in a working day? How many interviews should you be able to conduct during your shift? How long should it take to edit a tape? Be guided by whoever asks you to do the job, but remember that as you become more experienced, you should become more efficient and faster. Just make sure you meet your deadlines. Time management is all about being organised, so if you call anyone on the phone have your notepad and pen handy and, most importantly, all the details you need to pass on to your prospective interviewee, such as the time they will be on air, etc.

CHOOSING A CONTRIBUTOR

- Try not to be predictable. Remember that the listener can become bored if the same talking heads are wheeled on every time you want to discuss a particular subject – even if they are lively and knowledgeable individuals.

- Have a wide range of contacts in your files and continue to increase that range. Make a note of their area of expertise and how articulate they are on the phone, and whether you have heard them on air.

- Consider what preconceptions you are applying to your choice of interviewees.

- Think about what makes an acceptable microphone voice.

- Ask organisations to consider providing a spokesperson who is not your usual white male – a diversity of contributors should add variety to the range of questions you can ask and the range of answers you will hear.

- Consider the difference in viewpoint and spin on a subject you might obtain if you chose to interview someone older or younger, experienced or inexperienced, insider or outsider.

- You might also like to consider how you can avoid accusations that there is a pecking order when it comes to who is allowed to voice an opinion on the air. It can appear to some observers of the media that well-known figures and self-appointed experts are more likely to be invited to express their views on air than lesser known persons. Bear this in mind when you are canvassing views or offering interviews.

Exercise

Imagine the government has just announced proposals to ban fox hunting using hounds. Think about who, where and when you would want to interview on the subject for:

- a three-minute news package

- a live studio discussion

- a vox-pop

- a feature or documentary

Exercise

Using the following biographical details, devise a range of questions to put to the interviewee about her career. Aim for an in-depth interview that allows the interviewee to give the listener an insight into her personality, character, work and beliefs. Try to devise questions that will highlight the landmarks in her career. Explore the influences on her work and the motivation behind her writing. Think about questions that will provoke surprising answers and anecdotes. In a longer interview, remember that a logical order to your questions will shape the interview and aid listeners' understanding and ease of concentration.

Annie Hammond. Born in Aberdeen. Only child. Left school at 16. Employment includes film extra, cinema usherette and taxi driver. Recently divorced from soap actor husband. First novel based on the life of her great-grandmother who was a trapeze artist in a travelling circus. Latest publication, her fifth, is a collection of short stories on the theme of Scottish identity and has been nominated for a literary award. Failed to win a seat in the Scottish Parliament elections when she stood as an Independent candidate. Plans to set up a scheme to encourage young writers and help them get their work published.

WHAT YOUR INTERVIEWEE NEEDS TO KNOW

It is easy to forget to supply your potential contributor with the background and useful information they need in order to prepare for a successful interview. Often the inexperienced interviewee will be unaware that they may ask for such information to help put their message across effectively. More experienced interviewees or their staff may make unreasonable demands. It should be up to the person organising the interview to take the initiative, so keep this checklist near the phone when you are finalising details with your interviewee:

- Explain why you have asked them for an interview. They may feel that they are under-qualified or lack authority and want to suggest an alternative.

- Tell them who will be conducting the interview and for which programme. This will give them a chance to listen in if they have not heard the programme before, and get an idea of the content and interview style.

- Establish whether the interview will be in the studio, via telephone or on location. They may need directions or transport; they may be expected to provide appropriate clothing; they may need to provide alternative contact numbers or obtain instructions on how to access and operate unmanned studio equipment. They may decide, if the opposition are to be in the studio for the interview, to change their plans and attend at the studio instead of on the telephone.

- Supply a profile of the station or programme's audience. If the target audience is younger or older than expected, your interviewee may need to adjust the pitch of their answers and illustrative examples.

- Confirm just how long the interview will be, so that they can consider the pace and the duration of their answers. This can also save your guest wasting weeks researching in order to give unnecessarily full and lengthy answers. All potential interviewees are busy people; the interview will not be the only engagement in their diary, so the proposed duration is important. They may even suggest that they can only spare you five minutes when you have asked for ten. But after agreeing to the reduced time span, you may well end up spending half a day in conversation with them, because despite their fears that they might get bored or might not get on with you, they find themselves enjoying the experience.

- Outline the aim of the interview and the main points to be covered. It can be embarrassing for all concerned if the guest has prepared for an interview about the future of further education and finds themselves being asked about the techniques of candlemaking. But you should resist any requests to provide the actual questions, and any demands to be asked or not asked particular questions.

- Tell them whether the interview is to be live or recorded. This will affect their performance and stress levels if they are running late prior to arriving at the studio or location. Resist any requests or demands for the interview to be featured at a particular time slot in a programme.

- Interviewees need to be warned if there will there be a phone-in element. Unpredictable questions from an unpredictable interviewer, namely the radio listener, can throw even the most capable politician.

- You must tell them who else will be taking part in the interview. This means they can withdraw at this stage if they are not happy about the arrangements, rather than be surprised on arrival at the interview and walk out minutes before they should be on air. It also enables them to ascertain any opposing opinions or arguments other guests may intend to voice.

Other things an interviewee may want to know

An inexperienced interviewee may also ask you for tips on how to, for want of a better word, 'behave' on air. A common concern is how they should refer to the interviewer on air. Should it be first-name terms? How often should they use the name? Here are a few hints you can supply to aid the interviewee's performance:

- Arrive early, but do not be surprised if you only get the chance to have a few words with the interviewer before going on air, especially if you are part of a live programme.

- Avoid wearing any noisy jewellery in the studio and leave the bleeping watch at home. These noises will distract the listener.

- Switch off your mobile phone.

- Please do not swing around in your studio chair. If you do, the microphone will not pick up your voice properly.

- Try not to hit the microphone or kick the table, but don't be afraid to move your hands about when you are speaking.

- Speak at normal volume and directly to the interviewer. Don't try to address the listener unless they are taking part in a phone-in.

- When you have said what you want to say, stop speaking and let the interviewer ask you another question. Some interviewees try to get across all their points in their first answer.

- Be yourself, and if it is appropriate don't be afraid to smile.

- When the interview is over wait silently until the red light is off.

RESEARCH

As well as being so attached to their contacts book that it can appear to be an extra limb, the best and most efficient researchers also carry around a notebook and use it for jotting down any good ideas for interviews or topics that could feature in their programme. These ideas may come from the novel they are reading on the train into work, a poster they see on the street or something somebody says in the pub. They note down anything that they think they may be able to use in the future. Their research is ongoing, in other words they listen to as much radio as possible, and not just their own programme or station. If they hear a good speaker on the radio they take down the name and the subject under discussion in case they could be of use. They also rip out or photocopy particularly interesting articles in magazines or newspapers to keep for future reference or to stimulate ideas.

Within the time restraints of a deadline, you should try to get as much accurate and appropriate information as you can on the topic of your interview, and as much information about the person that you are going to interview and their views. Allocate your time wisely; there is no point in doing enough research for an entire documentary when the interview will only be used to be part of a wrap. If the contributor has a particular viewpoint on a subject, what are the views that they may disagree with? Subject-related publications, press cuttings and websites should get you started. Hunt out any videos on the subject, or if you have access to audio archives check out previous interviews that may have been broadcast. Once you have done the reading, start talking to people in relevant organisations, businesses, clubs and societies. Let colleagues know what you are researching, because unbeknown to you they may be able to provide useful information or even contacts of their own. Get to know the sources of information available to you – reference books like atlases, dictionaries and encyclopaedias; electoral registers, trade and specialist journals and publications, press cuttings, websites, etc. Get to know where these sources can be accessed otherwise you will waste valuable research time searching for them.

A preliminary telephone conversation with your interviewee is also advisable. This will give you a clearer insight into the subject and what they have to say about it. Be very clear about what it is you want to ask them, in order to avoid misunderstandings and a conversation that flies off on all sorts of tangents. Keep your questions simple at this stage, but don't take everything at face value and be prepared to politely challenge in a questioning way. You can encourage interviewees to illustrate what they have to say with anecdotes. Check any facts or information that you have discovered and compare them with your contributor's view of things. Even double-check that names and titles are correct. Be on the lookout for any new angles or revelations that may change the focus of the interview. Make careful notes during the conversation – this will help you to focus the interview and formulate the questions you will eventually use.

Once you have read, phoned and surfed all the obvious connections, remember to think about the less obvious sources of information.

One of my earliest assignments as a trainee reporter was tracking down and interviewing the 'matchstick man'. On my first day in a local radio newsroom, the duty editor gave me a clipping from the local evening newspaper about a man who had built a full-size knight in armour out of matchsticks. The editor wanted an interview with him for the drivetime programme going out later that day. Not only was it my first day at the station, but it was also my first day in the city. The clipping contained the man's name and the street where he lived, but no house number. The name was not listed in the phone book. Undeterred and determined to make my mark on my first day, I grabbed a tape recorder and a local map and drove off, only to find that the street was the longest residential street in the city. I cursed myself for not checking the electoral register before I left the station. I tried knocking on a few doors but nobody seemed to know where this chap lived; the corner shop was no help, nor the pub, nor the garage. However, the owner of a small tobacconist's shop knew all about him – after all, my man had had to buy his supply of matches from somewhere.

What should be included in a research brief?

The idea of a brief is to provide an interviewer with background information to enable them to conduct an interview. Whether you are expecting someone to do the research for you or doing it yourself, the brief should be broken down into concise sections, with facts in a logical order and a layout that makes the brief easy to read, easy to follow and easy to digest. Key points in the research information should be marked with a highlighter pen, written in capitals, or simply underlined. It is important to give details of any sources that you use, such as press releases, newspaper cuttings, extracts from a book or the transcript of a previous interview. Remember that statements made in a newspaper may be inaccurate or refuted in later editions, so double-check your sources. During the course of your research you might like to check and confirm the facts you have gathered with the interviewee when you talk through the interview with them. It is a good idea not to write down anything that you wouldn't want the interviewee to see or anything you wouldn't want them to say on air. Always allow time in your schedule to talk through the brief with the interviewer if they want to. If you are a one-person operation, it is still a good idea to produce a brief for yourself – it can do a lot to help focus the interview.

Everyone has their own system or preferred way of doing things, but until you develop your own or have to adopt those of your employer, here are a few suggestions for what should be included in the brief:

- name of researcher
- title, date and time of programme
- name of interviewer
- introduction summarising what the brief is about
- name of interviewee(s), including title, job, who they represent, etc.
- date and place of interview – with contact number, transport and parking arrangements, timetables, hotel booking, maps, etc.
- reason for interview – e.g. new book (include a copy), new film (attend a screening or enclose publicity and review material), arrival of a new comet (attach specialist magazine clippings)
- reason this person is being interviewed – e.g. author, film actor, astronomer
- background research material on
  - (a) the story, including any controversial angles or quotes
  - (b) the contributor, including biographical details and if appropriate a summary of their views, opinions and experiences of the subject under discussion; be selective and focused, but not dry
  - (c) what others have said about the subject
- details of attachments

From your research you should be able to make suggestions about areas to cover during the interview, but leave the choice of questions to the interviewer. It is equally important to suggest areas the interviewer should avoid because of possible libel, a currently pending court case, or subjects that may be too upsetting for the interviewee to discuss.

The interviewer may also be interested to hear about any impressions you may have formed during your conversations with the interviewee – but in the end the listener will only be interested in the on-air relationship between interviewer and interviewee.

Keep a copy of the brief for future reference and as useful research material.

Exercise

Try your hand at a bit of research for a radio programme by finding out as much relevant information as you can about one of the subjects in the following list. Prepare a brief for a reporter who is to be sent on location to conduct an interview for a weekly magazine programme about travel. You should decide who the interviewer will be interviewing.

- planning a literary tour of Hampshire

- the best way to spend a rainy day in York with two teenagers

- choosing an activity weekend on a limited budget

RISK OR HAZARD ASSESSMENT

No interview is worth injury or worse to interviewer, interviewee, or any bystander. The journalist's job is to get the story, not become it. Risk assessment is a crucial part of planning. Hazards that may arise should be identified in the early stages. If something does go wrong, at least you can argue you had thought about potential problems prior to the event and that you had been acting professionally and responsibly by implementing reasonable safeguards.

If there are any worries about potential danger to anyone involved in an interview, using a standard risk assessment form is the first step to avoiding injury. If there are any doubts then fill out the form and use it as a discussion document when planning the interview. Remember to keep a copy on file, and if details change after decisions have been made, complete another form before continuing with the planning.

- If you feel there is a possible risk or hazard, use a checklist to guide your risk assessment planning and keep a written log of your actions.

- Fill out a risk assessment form and discuss any potential hazards with your producer/editor.

- Decide how to eliminate or minimise any risks. This may just mean talking over changes to a location with the person responsible for the site of the interview. It may involve ensuring that everyone involved with the interview is aware of their individual responsibilities.

Risk assessment forms should be designed for individual organisations, but should contain the same basic information.

Risk assessment form

Name of interviewer ....
Programme or department ....
Date of interview ....
Location of interview ....
Details of interview ....
Person responsible for safety on location ....
Potential hazards identified ....
Potential risks to interviewer, etc. ....
Precautions proposed ....

Signed ....(Producer/Editor)

You are most likely to encounter problems when interviewing out on location. Wherever you go to conduct your interview, bear in mind that you may need to take protective or high-visibility clothing, headgear, ear- or eye protectors, masks, footwear, etc., or to borrow some when you arrive at the site. If you are recording outdoors, make sure you are suitably dressed and prepared for changes in the weather. Did you listen to the weather report? You may need permission to interview even in public places like railway platforms, and you may need to be accompanied by a representative from the site. Places of work like farms, factories, offices and shops may need to provide you with information about potential hazards, for example from vehicles, machinery, equipment or chemicals.

Consider also your suitability to attend a particular location. Do you suffer from any allergies that may be aggravated by contact with certain foods, chemicals or animals? Should you be conducting an interview in a hot-air balloon if you have a fear of heights? If you are pregnant or a new mother you are advised not to go to an area where animals have recently given birth.

Make sure you do not become the cause of more problems at the site of the interview. It may be necessary to refrain from smoking, to switch off a mobile phone or leave a site immediately if asked to do so. Do not distract workers, and always record at a safe distance from traffic, platform edges or work areas. At demonstrations or protest marches you should avoid having any influence or involvement, so be prepared to stop interviewing if your presence appears to change the behaviour or mood of the participants.

If you have to attend a major incident like a motorway accident or a fire on an industrial estate, the risks you may have to face are pretty obvious, but no two incidents will be the same. The main considerations are that you should not interfere with the operations of the emergency services, and should avoid any personal injury or causing injury to others. Make sure the emergency services know you will be attending and report to whoever is in charge when you arrive. Roads may be closed off or clogged with traffic because of the incident, so get some instructions on the best way to reach the site. Always follow any instructions given to you by the emergency services at the site.

It is important to discuss safety issues. Familiarise yourself with the radio station's procedures, so that if you need to attend an interview in a hurry you will not waste time checking what action you should be taking. Check your insurance cover at the same time.

Exercise

You have been asked by your editor to go to the site of some local roadworks that have had to be halted because a rare orchid has been found growing on the roadside verge. You will be interviewing a council representative and a botanist based at the local university.

Before you drive to the site, draw up a detailed list of the procedures you should follow and the questions you should be asking.

What precautions should you be taking to protect yourself from injury during the interview?

What can you do to contribute towards the safety of your interviewees and the public during the interview?

How would the assessment differ if

(a) the interviews are recorded on site with a portable recorder;
(b) the interviews are conducted live into a programme using the radio car?

Exercise

You have been given the job of interviewing the proud parents of the first baby to be born after midnight on New Year's Eve. Draw up a checklist of things you should do leading up to, during and after the interview at the local hospital, in order to get your interviews efficiently and safely.

How would your checklists differ if

(a) the interviews are recorded with a portable recorder?
(b) the interviews are conducted live into a programme using the radio car?

ASKING THE QUESTIONS

It is important that you spend some time deciding what questions you will ask and how you will word them. Your starting point should be to write down the one question you *must* ask your interviewee. This should be the most important question and the one that the listener wants the answer to, but never the question the interviewee wants you to ask. Underneath jot down a few more questions based on your top question. Follow these with a list of questions you *should* ask, and finally, if time will allow, some questions you *could* ask. In reality you are looking for three or four key questions, and to follow them up with supplementary questions based on the replies you receive from the interviewee.

Do not write out your questions in full. File them away in your mind and make a short list in note form, perhaps even one-word notes to act as a memory jogger at the interview. Be prepared to drop some of your questions if better ones are suggested by the answers your interviewee gives you.

To be most effective on air, keep your questions short and straightforward.

For a news story you have to ask your questions in a brisk and business-like way. Adjust and adapt your mood and manner for a lighter or sensitive interview.

If you are not getting the answers you want or do not get what you consider to be answers at all, then you could try asking the question again in a slightly different form.

Sometimes a statement before a question will indicate to the interviewee the way that your mind is working and put the question in context.

So if things are likely to go wrong, then why not solve the problems by having a rehearsal or run-through before the real thing? This is OK for a theatre performance where everyone has learned their lines, but the radio interview should sound spontaneous. By all means have a warm-up chat, but do not make it too long, or your interviewee will not sparkle during the interview – the adrenaline will be gone and the excitement lost, and the result will be a stale, lacklustre interview. The interviewee may even come out with an expression like 'As I was saying before ... ' and refer to something that was said before the interview started. They may omit to relate a brilliant anecdote because they think they have already told it during the interview, when in fact they told it to you during the warm-up chat.

Some practitioners suggest that the first question should be a throwaway that will just warm up the interviewee and get them relaxed. If it is a recorded interview then the answer can be edited out. If you are short of time or are conducting a live interview, make sure the first question is focused but open, and allows your interviewee to expand on the topic under discussion.

Do not be tempted to start one question with another, such as 'Can I start by asking you … ?' or 'Can I ask you … ?' or 'Could you tell us … ?' or to use the expression 'I would like to start by asking you … '.

Avoid suggesting or offering alternative answers for your interviewee to choose from, for example 'Did you choose a career in the theatre because your father was an actor or because you failed as a writer?'

Avoid non-questions. Always follow any statements that you make with a question.

Finally, avoid saying 'And finally … '. Another question may be necessary after the answer. Also, you may want to re-order the interview and you may find the final question and answer fits better elsewhere. Of course you can edit out the words, but why make more work for yourself? .

The final answer of the interview is important. You want the piece to end positively and not just fizzle out. Final questions could include one that asks the interviewee to sum up their attitude or feelings about the topic; it could be a 'future' question that asks for a prediction or insight to how things may develop; or it could be a question that demands a short, snappy or decisive answer.

Types of question

Asking the right question is essential and it helps if you know which type you need to use to elicit an appropriate answer.

- Open question: This is usually the most effective for radio interviews and research interviewing. It invites the interviewee to give an expansive reply. These questions will start with 'who', 'what', 'when', 'where', 'how' and most revealingly 'why'.

    - Who decides which route the by-pass should take?

    - What will the final cost of the by-pass be?

    - Where will the new road be built?

    - How will you convince local residents that this is the best route?

    - Why didn't the council consult with the residents' association earlier?

- Closed question: This type of question results in a yes/no answer. It's a favourite with lawyers in court but is not always suitable for radio interviews. If you do not want monosyllabic answers then it should be avoided. Reverse-verb questions like 'Is it ... ?' and 'Do you ... ?' will invite a yes or no answer. Most radio interviews require fuller replies, or at least ones that are longer than the question. There are occasions when a closed question is the only one to ask, for example 'Are you going to resign, Mr President?', or if you only have time for a short reply before the interview slot ends.

- Multiple question: For example, 'How will the route for the by-pass be decided and who is going to foot the bill?' This type of question has no place in a radio interview. If you ask more than one question at a time you will confuse both interviewee and listener. The interviewee is likely to answer the second part of the question because they have forgotten the first part, or they will deliberately answer the part they find easiest.

- Summary question: This is a useful method of asking a question and at the same time keeping the interviewee focused, of clarifying information and helping the listener to concentrate on the story. It involves the interviewer repeating part of the interviewee's last answer as a prelude to the next question: 'So we know the route of the new by-pass, we know how much it's going to cost. When will traffic be able to use it?'

- Probing question: Once the interviewee has revealed certain information, stated an opinion or expressed their feelings about a topic, it may be necessary to hear more details. The interviewer should ask questions beginning with phrases like 'Tell me more about ... ', 'Could you explain why ... ' and 'What was going around your mind when ... '.

- Confrontational question: The most direct questions are often the most challenging for the interviewee. They can give the impression that the interviewer is running out of patience and wants direct, no-nonsense answers. In practice, the interviewer is calling on the interviewee to be accountable for their actions or decisions – 'Do you admit that mistakes have been made in the council's handling of this issue?'

- Hypothetical question:

  - What do you think the residents will do when they hear that the waste site may be positioned a few metres from the estate?

  - If you lived on the estate, how would you react to this news about the waste site?

  - I know that we cannot discuss this particular case which is going through the courts at the moment, but what changes should be made to the law to prevent this kind of thing happening again?

- Leading question:

  - This decision by the council is obviously a mistake, isn't it?

  - It's clear that the council has made a mistake, so what are you going to do about it?

EXERCISE

Read the press release on page 84, which arrives on your desk the day it is issued. Then:

- Decide if it is worth covering. Should it be simply a couple of lines of copy in a bulletin, or is it worth arranging an interview? If you decide 'yes', how long an interview do you want? Enough for a clip or a wrap, or longer?

- Decide who you want to talk to. Should it be an elected member of the council or a council officer? What would you expect them to say if you interviewed them?

- Who is likely to oppose the scheme?

- Is there any interest in this story for a national audience, or is it only of local interest?

- Decide why you want to talk to your interviewee and what questions you want to ask.

- What type of question will you be asking (information gathering, expert opinion, etc.)?

- Is there potential for a vox-pop or phone-in?

- Would the story benefit from location interviews or would it be better studio-based?

- What is the best way to treat this story on air? Will you use your interviews for a clip, wrap or package, or simply gather information for a copy story?

- Will you rush to get this story on the air straight away?

- Is there any possibility of controversy arising from this story? We know it is topical and has a human interest angle, but what about conflict?

WESTFORD COUNTY COUNCIL
NEWS RELEASE
10 March (Embargo until after midnight 12 March)
Issued by the Press Liaison Officer, County Hall, Westford

County wins cash for CCTV in Stratworth

Stratworth town centre is to step up its fight against crime with the installation of new closed-circuit TV cameras.

This anti-crime initiative comes courtesy of a successful bid to the Government for funding. Westford County Council has secured £120,267 to place twelve cameras around the Stratworth town centre area.

Local businesses, residents and community groups will be consulted on the best positions for the new cameras. Work on the project will start next month and will take two years to complete.

ENDS.

Ref: AA/123
Press contact: Adam Smith

7
At the interview

FIRST IMPRESSIONS

When you meet your interviewee for the first time at the studio or on location, you will probably have very little time to build up a relationship, so settle for a rapport. Dress appropriately for the occasion, and in a way that reflects your professionalism; remember you are acting as a representative of your radio station or production company and the listener. Don't dress up or down to match the stereotypical image that you may have of your interviewee – this can appear to be patronising and does not truly reflect the relationship that you wish to nurture. At the same time you do not want to make your interviewee feel uncomfortable or make yourself feel out of place. I remember a colleague being sent out to conduct an interview with a group of nudists. He never did tell us if he had kept his clothes on. You should also be prepared for the unexpected. Many reporters who regularly interview on location always keep a pair of wellies in the boot of the car in case they are called out to a muddy or wet site, together with a safety hat. If you are male, keep a tie in the desk drawer to smarten up your appearance. Don't go overboard – the days are long gone when radio announcers had to wear evening dress at the microphone.

Make sure you know the route you will follow to get to your location interview, and allow extra time in case you take a wrong turning or miss a connection. If something happens that prevents you from attending an interview or delays your arrival, make sure you or someone from base lets your interviewee know that you will be late, and confirm that it will still be convenient for you to conduct the interview at a later time. If it is not convenient then a new date will have to be fixed. Whatever happens, never leave your interviewee in the dark or at worst stranded at a location.

MEETING AND GREETING

If you are meeting on location you should introduce yourself. Remind your interviewee who you represent and why you have come to talk to them. Avoid using the word interview at this stage – it may frighten them off.

After some small talk you should be ready to set up your recorder, but don't start recording straight away.

If the interview is being conducted in the studio it is up to you to make sure the interviewee is made to feel welcome.

Arrange for someone to meet your guest in reception and bring them to the studio, pointing out cloakroom facilities on the way.

Someone should remind the guest who will be interviewing them, which programme the interview is intended for, how long the interview will take, and who else may be taking part in the programme. This should be a reminder because all these points will have been made when the interview was being fixed.

IN THE STUDIO

This is your home ground and you feel comfortable here. Unless they are a regular contributor, your guest will feel as though they are entering the lion's den. A studio can be a distracting, confusing and noisy place for the inexperienced interviewee. However, a tour of the facilities may not be advisable at this stage as it is time-consuming and may frighten them even more.

- When they arrive, introduce yourself and sit them at their microphone.
- Make sure you have the cue sheet and any notes for the interview in front of you before you open the microphone.
- During the interview listen to what your guest is saying.

- Try to maintain eye contact, otherwise they may feel the interview has ended.

- Look interested in what they are saying and encourage them with nods of the head, smiles, etc.

- Keep an eye on the clock on the wall.

- Watch those voice levels by checking the meters and by monitoring what you hear.

LIVE STUDIO INTERVIEWS

Interviewing live from a radio studio is exciting. It can also be a little frightening, no matter how experienced you are at it. Timings are crucial if the interview is part of a longer programme. Make sure that the interviewee is given enough time to put over their point of view, and tailor the interview to allow it to come to an unhurried conclusion.

Live interviews can often provide unexpected incidents that the interviewer must cope with alone and on the spot. I still have nightmares about a snake that a local zoo keeper had brought into the studio to talk about in his weekly slot. The snake decided to slither inside the mixing desk during the interview. Luckily I had a record cued up to play to air whilst we extracted the snake from the equipment before it could be electrocuted. On another occasion a mynah bird insisted on using bad language and flicking bits of seed at me through the bars of its cage during a live interview with its owner.

It is important to let your guest know exactly what is going on in the studio.

- Remind the guest that this is a live interview.

- Explain that when the red light comes on, the studio is on air and anything said will be heard by the listener.

- Tell them that they will not need to wear headphones unless they are taking part in a phone-in or discussion with guests in another studio.

- If they have a telephone number or address that they want to pass on to the listener, make sure they have it written down in front of them. If they are nervous or flustered they may forget it or get it wrong.

- Take sound levels from your guest as you chat about their journey to the studio or something similar.

- Explain the procedure you intend to follow, for example 'When this record ends I must just read out some travel information, then I will introduce you and ask you my first question, is that OK?'

- Remind your guest about the general areas of questioning you will be covering, e.g. 'I shall be asking you questions about your job as an Elvis impersonator, why you admire Elvis, the songs you choose … '.

- Tell your guest the first question you intend to ask them so that they can focus their attention and not dry up when you open their microphone.

- If you are expecting your studio guest to respond or react to the views of another guest or a report that is on tape, play the tape to them before going on air to give them an opportunity to prepare their response.

- Ask them to turn away from the microphone if they need to cough or clear their throat – you do not want to deafen the listener.

- Warn them that during the interview you may have to look away sometimes to check that everything is working OK or to write down some information that you receive in the headphones. Ask them to carry on as though nothing is happening.

- Ask them to stay quietly at the microphone once the interview has ended, and say you will tell them when the microphones are no longer live.

RECORDED STUDIO INTERVIEWS

In addition to the above guidelines:

- Remember to load the recorder with sufficient blank tape, cassette, disk, etc.

- Before opening the microphone put the machine into record mode and check it is recording.

- This is a recording, so interview with editing in mind.

- Do not let your guest leave the studio until you have checked that the interview has been recorded.

- Label your recording.

RECORDING ON LOCATION

One of the main reasons for choosing to record a contributor on location is to use the background or ambient noise to add atmosphere and a sense of place to the interview. You are bringing the sounds of the outdoors to the listener.

It is important to take time and care to make sure you come back to the studio with the best quality recording possible. As well as listening to the voice of your interviewee when you record the interview, make sure you listen out for changes in the background noise, or any intrusion and or sudden noises which detract from what is being said. For these reasons you should wear headphones – you may feel you look silly, but remember you are working and must bring back well-recorded material. Wearing headphones will ensure you always hear what the microphone is picking up. Be prepared to record your questions and answers again if they are affected by extraneous noise. Always record with editing in mind.

OUTDOOR LOCATION RECORDING

Arrive early and listen to the sounds of the location.

Is the roar of the traffic too loud?

- Move to a side street. You will still hear the traffic on the recording but it won't drown out your contributor's words.

Do aeroplanes pass overhead regularly?

- Warn your contributor that you may stop and start recording the interview to minimise interference and difficult editing.

Is there a busker performing nearby?

- As well as causing you problems when it comes to editing the interview because the music is part of the background noise, they may also demand a performance fee, and you could have copyright problems.

Will you need to find shelter out of the wind?

- If you can't, then stand with your back to the wind. It may even be necessary to hold up one side of your open coat or an umbrella to act as a windbreak and avoid that characteristic 'thumping' noise on your recording. If you have forgotten your windshield, tie a handkerchief or similar loosely around the microphone.

Record half a minute of wildtrack (raw background noise from the location) at the start and finish of the interview. This will give you a choice of material to blend in to the interview during a studio mix. It will be useful to disguise any audible edits which occur when the original background noise has been recorded at too high a level. Buses and lorries that were passing can suddenly appear or disappear when you remove a word or sentence.

SETTING LEVELS

- If you want to pick up ambient noise on your recording, then you should hold the microphone back a little from your contributor and turn up the recording input levels.

- To avoid recording some of the ambient noise, then you should hold the microphone closer to your contributor and turn down the recording input levels. Position yourself with your back to the noise and the contributor facing it so that the microphone points away from the noise, for example, in a crowded room.

- If your interviewee speaks more quietly than you, position the microphone closer to them or position it further from yourself when you speak to keep the sound balanced.

INDOOR LOCATION RECORDING

- As with outdoor locations, you may want to avoid some background noise. It is a good idea to arrive early and listen to the room where you will conduct the interview. Is there a clock ticking, a phone likely to ring, air conditioning or a refrigerator likely to suddenly switch on or off? All of these could at worst disrupt your recording. At the very least they will cause you editing problems. In offices, photocopying machines and computers can cause interference on your recording.

- If you are in a big room that echoes, position your interviewee with their back to the edge of the room – preferably near some closed curtains to absorb the echo. You should stand with your back to the rest of the room. Hold the microphone close to the interviewee and reduce the recording input level. Remember that putting the microphone closer to the interviewee may be intimidating for them, so ask them if it is OK.

- Conducting your interview in a small room could result in a muffled recording. To avoid this, try opening the door or window to give the impression of a larger space.

- Sit or stand alongside your interviewee, not directly in front of them. Touching knees can be an invasion of personal space, and being face on is more confrontational. Position yourself so that you can cradle the arm holding the microphone. You will be surprised how quickly your arm will start to ache or go numb when it is held steady in one position. This can be very distracting.

- Avoid interviewing across a desk. Not only will you have to stretch across a space, but the sound of your voices will be reflected off the hard surface and give a poor recording.

- Once you feel that the room is satisfactory, remember to record some wildtrack – even an empty, seemingly silent room has acoustics. Start your recording of the background sounds from the same spot where you will conduct the actual interview, and at the same recording input level you will be using for the interview. This will give you natural-sounding material. If you are not happy with the room you have been allocated, explain why and ask if it is possible to move to a more suitable location.

Think about the potential and the pitfalls of conducting an interview in each of the following locations:

- an open field

- a public house

- a church

- a livestock market

RECORDING THE INTERVIEW

- Position the recorder to your side or in front of you. You will need to check the meter and perhaps adjust levels during the recording, so it should be within easy reach. Do not place it too close to the microphone or you may pick up the hum of the machine over your recording.

- Hold the microphone at chin level, about 12–15cm from your contributor. The microphone should be at a slight angle so that the contributor speaks down and across, and not directly into it. If the microphone is too close and pointed directly at the mouth of the speaker, you will hear a 'popping' sound on your recording, especially with 'p' or 'b' consonants.

- Check your own level – unless you are planning to edit out your voice from the piece. Take your contributor's level by getting them to say a few words. Ask them their name and position, as it will be useful to have it on tape when it comes to writing the cue and using correct pronunciation in your links. Get the level right before you start the interview and you will be able to concentrate on listening to what is being said.

- Handle the microphone with care to avoid noise being transferred through its main body, connectors or cable. It is best to wind some of the microphone lead around your hand so that any movement does not disturb the connections, which can produce a noise on your recording known as 'mike rattle'. If you wear a ring be aware that the sound of it tapping on the side of the microphone will also be heard on your recording. Try to keep the microphone still to reduce the risk of rattle, but obviously if your interviewee moves about then you need to follow their mouth to pick up what is being said.

- To add extra zip to your interviews, consider the possibility of conducting the interview on the move. Certainly, the interview with the marathon runner as he jogs along may end up being of short duration and full of wheezing from the interviewer, but a gentle stroll through an art gallery or along a garden path can add character to the conversation. Watch out for mike rattle and avoid it by keeping your microphone as steady as possible. You may also like to consider recording the interview in mono and some wildtrack in stereo. Mix them back at the studio and you will have a fuller, more atmospheric outdoor feel to your interview.

- During the interview check the level meter is still registering correctly, without distracting your interviewee, as you need to maintain eye contact and look interested.

- Encourage your interviewee with nods and smiles, but avoid irritating asides like 'I see', 'Mmm' and 'Uh-huh', which you will have to edit out if you don't want the listener screaming at the radio demanding that you shut up.

- Remember this is a recording so you can stop and start it or do a retake of a question or answer.

- Be careful not to record too much material. You will create editing problems for yourself if you have to reduce thirty minutes of recording into a two-minute package. Your interviewee will feel justifiably disappointed when they hear the end result on air.

- Ask the interviewee if there is anything else they want to say, add or tell you. This gives them the opportunity to correct anything they or you may have said, and cover any points you may have inadvertently forgotten to discuss.

- At the end of the interview resist the temptation to play the whole piece back to your contributor. They will only want to change it. But you should rewind and play back the last few seconds to confirm you have recorded the interview. If you need to retake any of your stumbled or convoluted questions, now is the time to do it, not when you return to the studio. Later on they can be edited into their appropriate position in the piece.

- Label your recording with details of the interviewee, date and place of interview.

LIVE LOCATION INTERVIEWS

Live interviews from a location are usually conducted from a radio car or van from the scene of an incident or event, and perhaps a mobile studio at an agricultural show or sports event.

- If possible check that you are able to transmit a strong signal back to base before the event by arranging a test transmission before you book your guest.

- Choose your site for the radio car carefully. If you are surrounded by buildings your signal may be blocked. Watch out for the branches of trees or overhead cables that may inhibit the transmitter aerial when it is extended – you could find yourself in great danger if those cables are carrying electricity.

- Remember the extra height of the vehicle with that aerial on the roof when you drive into car parks with height barriers or height restrictions.

- Once on site follow the instructions given to you by the radio station concerning the operation of equipment.

- Take preventative measures to avoid anyone tripping over any cables that you may have to run across the ground. Use gaffer tape on dry hard surfaces, and rubber mats to cover and mark the route of the cables.

The advice on conducting live location interviews is the same as those for recorded interviews, but remember you will not be able to edit or mix the interview before transmission. If you are broadcasting into a live programme, the station will feed the output to you via your headphones so you will hear the hand-over to you from the programme presenter. Sometimes arrangements are made for the presenter or interviewer back in the studio to interview the guest on location. In such a case the interviewee needs to wear the headphones and hold the microphone.

GETTING THE BEST FROM YOUR INTERVIEWEE

All relationships are built on trust. The relationship between interviewer and interviewee is no different. Your interviewee has to be sure that you are the sort of person they want to open up to. You may need to spend more time establishing the relationship before you feel the time is right to start the interview. You will eventually find out what works for you, and you will develop your own methods and techniques to get the best out of your interviewee.

Interviewees come in all different shapes and sizes, which doesn't matter on radio because the listener can't see them, but what does matter is the amount of interviewing experience they have had. Some people are regularly interviewed as part of their professional life, such as entertainers and police officers. A high-profile interviewee, like a politician or spokesperson for a company in the public eye, may receive training in handling the media and be given advice on how to get their message across during interviews. They are also likely to want to have their ex-journalist press officer in attendance during the interview. Such interviewees can be a bane or a blessing. At best they will be able to put their message across, sound spontaneous and be less nervous in front of the microphone; at worst they will over-prepared, cautious and rehearsed. If you feel they are simply quoting the party line and giving stock answers, then throw in an appropriate surprise question. Asking the Minister for Education if she knows her thirteen times table, or the Minister of Sport to explain the offside rule, can produce some interesting reactions.

On the other hand, for a member of the public it may be the first and only time they are interviewed. They are likely to be unsure of themselves, nervous, and may try too hard to please; but others seem to be able to perform quite naturally.

Remember that by agreeing to be interviewed by you, an interviewee is licensing you to publish what they say, so nothing that is said can be considered to be off the record.

COPING WITH DIFFICULT INTERVIEWEES

Your interviewee is asking for the questions in writing in advance of the interview.

- Explain that this cannot be done because you don't know exactly what questions you will be asking or the order you will ask them in, as a lot will depend on the answers they give. However it will probably help them to know the topics you hope to cover and the sort of questions you will be asking. Never let the interviewee dictate the questions to be asked. However, if they suggest one that you think is important and that had not occurred to you, then by all means use it.

Your interviewee gives brief answers to your questions and you would like longer ones.

- Encourage them by saying 'That's interesting, please tell me more' or 'Could you explain how that came about?' You could also try playing the waiting game. Sit still and just look at them. If you do not speak, they will eventually. Once they do start, remember to nod encouragement. If it is a recording then the awkward silences can be edited out. It takes courage to use this technique if your interview is live.

Your interviewee seems unwilling to part with information.

- Perhaps they do not know the answers to the questions you are asking, so give them the opportunity to check the information. However, if you suspect evasion then it is your duty to expose it. If the interviewee is being deliberately vague, it is up to you to convince them that it is in everybody's interest to hear the full story.

Your interview is talking nineteen-to-the-dozen and you want to interject with a question or end the interview.

- Look at your interviewee, hold up a finger and at the same time open your mouth as if to speak and take a breath. Your guest will probably stop mid-sentence. If they have meandered away from the subject under discussion, try another question prefaced with, for example, 'Can we just go back to the strike? You were saying that ... '.

Your interviewee insists on answering your questions from a script that they have prepared.

- Try to avoid this situation before the interview starts by asking them not to do so. This may have to be mentioned during the fixing phone call stage, or when they suddenly place an eight-page document in front of them when they sit down at the microphone. If they have been warned off and still read verbatim, then gently remove the script when you are asking the next question.

Your interviewee is using terms or jargon the average listener may not understand.

• Ask your interviewee to explain these, or if you know them interject to explain briefly and then allow them to continue.

Your interviewee does not directly answer your questions.

• If they are deviating, simply say 'That's an interesting point, but what I think is more important for our listeners to know is … '.

  If they are avoiding the issue, try saying 'But it's a bit more complicated than that, isn't it?', followed by your question.

  If they are evading the question, try asking the question again. If they still don't answer to your satisfaction, ask again but preface the question with the words 'I'm sorry, but I want to get this clear … '.

  If they continue to avoid the issues you want to raise, you may have no choice but to confront them and ask why they will not answer your questions.

Your interviewee keeps asking you questions.

• You could try saying: 'Well, my views are not what the listener wants to hear right now, but I am sure they would like to hear what you think … '.

The interview turns into an argument.

• If you are doing your job properly it should not deteriorate into one, but make sure it's not your fault and stand your ground; stay firm but stay pleasant. Do not base your comments on personal opinion, but use statements and questions that are backed up with facts and figures. If the argument is between two contributors with opposing views, then as long as you remain in control of the interview and allow both sides a fair share of the air-time, do not worry about it.

Your interviewee demands to listen to the interview after recording in case they want to make changes.

- If there is time and you feel inclined to do so, then by all means play back the interview – but on the understanding that they will not be able to make any changes. You will be editing the tape before it goes on air, so naturally you will tidy up those coughs, splutters, pauses, expletives, ums and ers, etc.

  If you do not want to play it back, explain that your batteries in the recorder have a limited life and you may have another interview to record and don't want to use up the power by playing back. You could also insist you are already late for another interview/deadline and do not have enough time.

  If the interview is for broadcast try to let them know when it will be going out on air.

Your interviewee insists that their press officer or similar associate be present during the recording or broadcasting of the interview.

- Agree, but on condition that they do not interrupt or interject during the interview. If your interviewee wants to stop the recording at any point to consult their colleague about the answer they will give, you should, within reason, allow this to happen.

Your interviewee is noticeably nervous or shy during the interview and is finding it difficult to express themselves.

- If it is a recorded interview, stop and take a few minutes to try and relax them – just letting them stand up and walk around for a minute can help. Coaxing on air is acceptable – try saying 'take your time'. It is important that you are always in control, but supportive. You may find that you will need to ask more questions than usual, and perhaps precede them with informative statements to lead your interviewee in the direction you feel they need to go.

Your guest has a hoarse voice or a cough.

• It may be necessary to draw the listeners' attention to these facts at the start so that they are not distracted from what is being said in the interview. Before the interview ask your guest to turn away from the microphone if they need to cough or clear their throat to avoid deafening the listener and you. Make sure there is a glass of water handy for your guest.

Your interviewee uses bad language during the course of answering a question.

• Unlike television, there is no nine o'clock evening watershed for radio, but it is important to be sensitive about scheduling. It is a matter of judgement, but it may be necessary to give a bad language warning before the interview is broadcast, or to drop the interview. If the interview is being recorded, you must decide whether or not to leave the offending word or words in, depending on whether it will be a problem for your particular audience, or whether to remove the word and replace it with a 'bleep' to indicate that swearing did occur and you want to draw attention to the fact. Incidentally, if you choose this option, whatever sound you choose to replace the word, make sure the duration of this sound is the same as the word – this way you will not change the pace or rhythm of the piece. You may decide to remove the word and not replace it because it can be edited out without the listener hearing the edit. You may decide to stop the interview and retake the question and answer.

If the interview is live you must be careful not to draw attention to the error with profuse apologies or embarrassed silence. This has only happened to me once, when one of my guests in a studio interview, who is now himself an interviewer with a weekly chat programme on BBC Radio 4, was giving an enthusiastic reply to a question and a four-letter word slipped out. He realised at once what he had said, quickly added 'sorry about that', and carried on with his answer. No panic, no harm done and no listeners complained. If your interviewee does not apologise, it is up to you to decide whether to let it go by or to apologise to the listener yourself, by applauding your guest's enthusiasm, but not their choice of language. If your interviewee deliberately uses a string of expletives on air, I suggest you close their microphone and move on to your next item. Remember you have a responsibility within the areas of taste and decency to make sure that nothing offensive is broadcast.

Your interviewee makes a factual error during the interview.

- To correct or not to correct? If you correct your interviewee it could embarrass them, and if you don't the listener will be on the phone to the studio. Obviously, if it is a recorded interview you can stop, point out the error and then retake the question and answer again. If something is said during a live broadcast, you do not have this option. If, during an interview with an art historian or critic, they refer to 'Gainsborough's painting *The Haywain*' instead of 'Constable's painting *The Haywain*', then, because you expect them to have expert knowledge, you would assume it was a slip of the tongue and you might choose to ignore it. Would you do the same if the error was made by someone not involved in the world of art? I would suggest that all mistakes should be corrected immediately, politely and with as little fuss as possible. Make sure of your facts before you make any corrections, otherwise you may end up being embarrassed yourself.

You are interviewing a group of people and they all try to speak at the same time.

- Explain that to hear all their voices at once is confusing for the listener, who will not be able to make out what is being said. In a live studio interview, explain the rules before you go on air, and tell them that you will point at the person you want to speak and, if anyone else wants to make a comment, they should attract your attention by holding up their hand. If you are interviewing on location, ask your question directly to one person and point the microphone at them so there can be no misunderstanding about who should offer a reply. Give everyone in the group a chance to have their say, because you can edit out the replies you do not need.

PRESS CONFERENCES

A press conference could be a small gathering of local journalists receiving the low-down about the launch of a new road safety initiative, or a massive media scrum involving the world's press fighting to talk to a VIP. On the whole they tend to be routine and predictable, but useful occasions. They tend to be called if someone thinks there is enough press interest in the person, story or latest development to justify staging one.

Organisers of press conferences are aiming to cater for the needs of all the media representatives who attend, and to blitz them with their message in one fell swoop. The advantage to any organisation or individual holding a press conference is that they set the parameters, and are therefore in control. Many press agents and PR companies feel that if they organise a press conference they can subject their charges to a single onslaught in a relatively short time. Some feel that staging a media event will increase the amount of publicity they receive.

Press packs of information and data or press releases are usually issued before the start of proceedings, giving reporters little time to digest the material before deciding what questions to ask.

Many junior reporters are nervous about attending press conferences. They can be overawed by the occasion, worried about getting protocol wrong and being laughed at if they ask a question. At your first press call or conference you may want to adopt a listen-and-watch policy, which will help you learn the ropes, avoid any *faux pas* and perhaps hear some questions and answers you may be able to use yourself later. However, you should remember that you too have an agenda. You need to come back with a story worth telling, so take control. If you feel there is a question to be answered then ask it.

Recording an interview at a press conference can be a pain for the radio journalist. All the newspaper journalist has to do is make their notes and they have enough material for their story; the press photographer can snap away; and the TV film crew can probably manage with a few shots of the scene and a bit of the speaker performing. As a radio journalist you need those voices on tape. The temptation is to place your microphone on the table in front of the speaker. This technique is fine for print journalists collecting material that they will be transcribing later, but for you the result may be a recording that sounds off-mike, features other conversations even more off-mike, includes the sound of water being poured into glasses, etc., and is not a good enough quality for broadcast. However, you should do it anyway because it is a useful standby in case you don't get anything else. You may also decide to place your microphone in front of the public address loudspeaker in the room. Again, a technique not recommended except in emergencies, as the quality is usually poor. Finding the correct distance away and best level for the recording input can be a matter of trial and error. So why not position yourself in front of the speaker and get your microphone as close to them as possible? You may find television and photographer colleagues shouting at you to get your head out of their picture, and in order to oblige you will end up lying uncomfortably in an undignified position on the floor and find it impossible to ask any questions from there.

Try to negotiate, preferably in advance, a separate short interview with the most relevant spokesperson straight after the conference. The organisers can only say no, and probably will if the conference features a high-profile speaker, a personality or an overwrought victim they feel protective towards. Television journalists will probably ask for the same thing and want to go first if interviews are being held. They will argue that they have a deadline to meet which, if they miss it, will mean the material will not be broadcast; that tying up their equipment is expensive and they cannot wait around; that they have another assignment to travel to and anyway they will only take five minutes to do their filming. Some of these arguments hold water, but the last does not.

MEDIA SCRUMS

These are best avoided if you need to get an interview with someone. Try to make an appointment or attend an organised press conference. If there is no alternative and you just need a clip, a soundbite or a shouted remark, then get in there and get what you can. Expect damage to yourself and your recording equipment in the scramble. Decide on how you intend to behave if violence is threatened. If you intend to record an interview outside a law court, remember not even radio journalists are allowed to take tape recorders into court buildings, even if they promise to leave them switched off. Most radio stations have plastic tags or labels with their logo and name printed on that can be attached to a microphone. This helps interviewees know who is taking an interest in them, and to pinpoint particular interviewers. If there are TV cameras filming the event, the labels also offer a free advertising opportunity if you can get your microphone into shot.

On occasions it can be helpful to all concerned at a major event to pool information between members of the press and media and allow, for example, the emergency services to get on with their jobs or for victims of accidents or crimes to avoid a barrage of jostling cameras and microphones being pushed into their faces.

I was once called out to report on a riot at a local prison. When I arrived some buildings were alight and prison staff had been evacuated, but because the prisoners were running amok the fire brigade were not allowed inside to tackle the fire. I interviewed the fire chief and the prison governor about the situation. I realised that I was the only journalist at the scene. By the time others arrived, anyone in authority was too preoccupied to talk to the press until the press conference arranged for a couple of hours' time. I played the interviews I had recorded to anyone who asked to hear them and they made notes about what had been said so that they had the background information. What I did not mention was that I also had an interview with a resident who lived nearby. He had been walking his dog near the prison and witnessed a couple of prisoners escaping over the fence. Naturally he informed the police at the scene, but I had an exclusive interview for my newsroom and was not prepared to share it.

INTERVIEWING CORRESPONDENTS

Correspondents come in all flavours these days, each specialising in their own particular field – education, industry, health, transport, media, etc. Their job is to file stories about their specialist area, usually in the form of copy, a voicer, a wrap or a package. They also get asked to produce features and documentaries. Occasionally they are called upon to be at the receiving end of a live interview during a news programme. These interviews are commonly known as two-ways. The correspondent will know the questions in advance because they are based on the information they have already told the editor or producer on the piece just played into the programme. Sometimes the correspondent will be in the studio with the interviewer, but usually the interview takes the form of a live link between the reporter in the field and the studio newsreader/presenter asking for the latest on the situation, followed by questions designed to get an analysis of events so far, speculation about how they will progress, and an informed guess about the possible outcome or resolution. This slightly disingenuous technique can sound stage-managed, and at worst even contrived and lacking authority.

Correspondents on the spot are expected to offer up the next episode of the story and speculate on the future developments. They are expected to give informed but not expert opinion.

The questions they are likely to be asked can be limited and it sometimes appears as if they are being asked the same sort of question no matter what the story is:

- What is the situation at this moment from your point of view?

- What is likely to happen next – will things get worse before they get better?

- What is the likely outcome?

These questions can be applied to stories about union negotiations, the effects of a rail strike, the site of an unexploded bomb, a street demonstration, a row over exam results, etc.

If you are going to be on the receiving end of the interviewer's questions, then be prepared to add something new to what you have already reported – after all there must be a reason for coming back to you after you have filed your story.

INTERVIEWING PEOPLE IN POSITIONS OF AUTHORITY

In the early days of radio broadcasting, prominent figures were simply asked if they would 'like to say a few words for the microphone'. Long gone are the days when politicians and the like were treated with deference and allowed to say what they wanted without being questioned, yet alone challenged, by the radio interviewer. At the Radio Festival in 1999, radio presenter and interviewer Nicky Campbell described political interviewing on *Today* as a 'kind of verbal wrestling match'. Politicians accept that radio offers them the opportunity to speak directly to the voter in their own home; and that they are at a grave disadvantage if they are not prepared to participate in interviews and discussions. Once they understood that an interactive style of communication was required, they learnt how to perform better on air. Some politicians have now become adept at speaking on any subject at any time, and are regularly wheeled in as 'talking heads'. So media-aware are the politicians and others in positions of power and influence that they make sure they are fully briefed by researchers and advisors before attending an interview. They want to appear to speak with authority and leave the right message about their policies and personality in the ear of the listener. However, their media awareness has also enabled them better to avoid answering awkward questions and adopting techniques that give the impression that they are being constantly interrupted, so that the listener thinks they are being treated badly by the interviewer. As an interviewer you have the duty to highlight evasion. Your job is to get answers, so try posing the question again, but use different wording or approach the subject from a different point of view: 'Minister, what is your department doing to solve the problems of congestion on our roads?' 'Minister, what needs to be done to solve the problems of traffic congestion?' 'Minister, what assurances can you give motorists that something will be done to sort out the congestion on the roads?' 'Minister, what can we learn from other countries that are not experiencing these problems?' You could try summarising what the politician is saying, or not saying, and putting it back to them, for example, 'So, Minister, the roads of Britain are almost at gridlock and public transport is in a shambles, but at the moment your department is unable to take any short-term action to ease the problems. Is that in essence the situation?'

You could also try simply asking the same question over and over until you get an answer. This technique was used on the then Prime Minister Edward Heath, who was being questioned about his opposite number Harold Wilson. The interviewer asked Mr Heath three times 'Do you like him?' and never received a straight yes or no answer. More recently, Jeremy Paxman interviewed the then Home Secretary and asked him fourteen times if he had ever threatened to overrule decisions made by the Chief Inspector of Prisons. Paxman was later to insist that he only did it because the following item on the programme had fallen through and he had been told to keep the interview going.

Every now and then, one political party or another will accuse radio and television interviewers of being partial, aggressive, intrusive, biased, etc., particularly as an election looms or if election results were unfavourable; but if at the end of the year the bouquets and brickbats from both sides balance out, then you are probably getting it right.

Do not be overawed by the prospect of interviewing someone influential. The late Brian Redhead told me over lunch one day that he had conducted a live interview with Margaret Thatcher when she was Prime Minister in the back of the BBC News radio car which was parked outside 10 Downing Street. Nothing unusual about this, except that it was immediately after the results of a very important by-election had been announced in the early hours and, according to Brian, much to his surprise the PM climbed into the back seat wearing her nightdress and gown. This anecdote illustrates that we are all human, the importance of trust between interviewer and interviewee, the ability of radio to get immediate reaction to an event on the air and, of course, the advantage to the interviewee that radio is an invisible medium; after all the PM would not have appeared for a TV or print interview dressed that way.

If you find yourself in the position of interviewing a high-profile contributor, then remember you are a professional doing a job. Simply prepare, organise and communicate as you would for any interview, and you will get your material. Do not feel under pressure if your interviewee's advisors, personal assistants, press officers, etc. try to influence the questions you ask or the editing decisions you make. You should call the shots: don't be rude, just be assertive, and make sure they understand that you must be allowed to do your job, which is to secure a broadcast interview.

DEALING WITH THE PUBLIC

We interview people because we hope they will have something to say about a subject or themselves that will enlighten, entertain or advise us. A member of the public tends to be sought out by interviewers if they are an ordinary person who has done, seen or said something out of the ordinary, or had something out of the ordinary happen to them. In other words they have a story to tell, either about themselves or about something they witnessed. Being interviewed for the radio is a big deal for many people, so they will get quite worked up about it. They will be excited, wary and nervous all at once, so make it as easy as you can for them by dealing with their queries as carefully and directly as possible. It is not part of their job to make themselves accessible to the media, so help them to deliver what they want to say, but do not be any less rigorous in your line of questioning. They may relax once they discover it is just you and your tape recorder, not a whole crew of technicians. Individuals are also chosen because they match up to type and can be seen to be representative of others. Someone asked to take part in an interview may see this as their few minutes of fame, and exploit the situation by saying something sensational, simply to make an impact and get themselves noticed by others. If, as an interviewer, you are seeking out a range of views, it may be tempting to put words into the mouths of your interviewees. This is a temptation to be avoided. Only broadcast what you know or believe to be true.

Quite often you will be invited to conduct the interview in someone's home. This may make you feel a little uneasy. Generally, it is a good idea to let your guard down as much as possible and be like a neighbour who has popped around for a visit. Break the ice by accepting the offer of a cup of tea – it puts the meeting on a more everyday, comfortable level. Try to feel at home in their space. Chat about the garden, the budgie, and so on, but do not judge the person by their surroundings, and certainly do not let them sense any disapproval of their situation.

INTERVIEWING PERSONALITIES

Celebrities come in all sorts of guises, such as actors and authors, who regularly provide interview material on radio programmes when they have a product or performance to promote. However, after doing the rounds of the radio stations to do the honours and tell their life stories, they can sound bored when they are expected to answer the same question for the umpteenth time. So for their sake and yours and, it follows, for the sake of the listener, mix in a couple of surprises. Not questions that just appear randomly out of the blue, but questions which fit into the flow of the interview, based on the reply to a previous question. For example:

- Had you experienced anything like that before?

- When was the last time you felt like that?

- What would you have been if you hadn't become … ?

- What comes first for you – is it your work or your friends?

- What are you like to work with?

- What do you like/hate most about your job?

Illustrative material, like an extract from the archives of one of their classic performances or an extract read from their novel or autobiography, followed by a pertinent question, can get things going. If you find that the interview is just not sparkling because your interviewee sounds bored, try questions like these, followed by others based on the replies:

- What items do you always take with you when you leave the house?

- What book is on your bedside table?

- How do you want people to remember you?

A journalist who wrote a showbusiness column for a daily tabloid news-paper told me that he always kept the question 'When did you last cry?' up his sleeve in case he felt the interviewee was just fobbing him off with the standard answers to his questions.

Often you will find that an actor may have been on stage for two perfor-mances the day before, and you have asked them in for an interview before ten in the morning when they are not at their best; acknowledge this. You may find that if you seem to be interested in them and are really pulling out the stops to make the interview a success, then they will try that little bit harder. The important thing they need to be sure of is the focus of the interview. Is it to concentrate on their latest film or theatre role, or will you be covering their career to date? Will you be playing records to break up the interview, or is it all to be covered in one hefty lump?

If it is a general, all-encompassing interview, then try to seek out some lightweight topical responses. For example, if it's a cold/hot day ask about their favourite way to keep warm/cool. If Valentine's Day is close ask about what they find romantic, who was their first love, about their first kiss. If someone in the news has lost a winning lottery ticket, ask your guest what was their biggest disappointment.

These sorts of questions will increase the value of the interview and move away from the purely promotional element that is bound to be part of the agenda and offered as the *raison d'être* for the invitation to appear on the programme. Although a hook or peg for any interview is important, it can be less of a requirement in this situation.

Longer interviews can sometimes seem like relentless interrogation because of the question/answer rhythm, so offer some light and shade by balancing out serious and lighter areas of discussion.

You may also come across celebrity interviewees who wish to be inter-viewed 'in character'. I remember when the actors who created 'Hinge and Brackett' were touring theatres in the UK with a variety show and would only agree to give interviews on local stations in their stage personas. Obviously they saw these interviews as a promotional opportunity. They arrived at the studio without costume or make-up, but appeared on air using the voices of their characters. During breaks in the programme for music, they chatted to the interviewer in their everyday voices.

Offered such an interview, you may feel this would undermine its value because it would not reveal more about the person behind the character. You may decide that conducting the interview would compromise your reputation as an interviewer in the eyes of the listener. You may feel uncomfortable about appearing to be part of the publicity machine, and refuse interviewees who have something to plug. On the other hand you may decide that it could work in your favour, and produce a change from the usual run-of-the-mill interview. If an actor wants to appear in character, it may indicate that they feel more comfortable in their other skin. They may be able to say things they would not wish to say if they were themselves. Certainly, for news or short-reaction interviews, this can add impact. For example, the alter-ego of Barry Humphries, 'Dame Edna Everage', being interviewed on the results of a referendum in Australia on whether to keep the British monarchy or become a republic is bound to be a winner.

The choice comes down to the role the interview will play in the output of the station. Is the context appropriate? Will it tell the listener anything new?

As a footnote to this section, be aware that, if you are interviewing an entertainer or similar in their dressing room backstage at a concert hall or theatre, or even in a hotel room, you may have to be discreet about some of your interviewee's unguarded behaviour to which you may be unwisely exposed.

INTERVIEWING RELATIVES AND FRIENDS

There are very few programme makers or reporters who have not at some time or another conducted a broadcast interview with one of their nearest and dearest. It shouldn't happen on a regular basis or simply because they are at hand or because you couldn't be bothered to find a legitimate interviewee. Reporters who need just one more female voice for their vox-pop, or one more elderly voice expressing dissatisfaction about the increase in bus fares, may sometimes take this option. There have even been cases of reporters coaching a friend to state a particular opinion, in order to balance out the short and unidentified replies in a vox-pop. I do not condone this method of working, but I can understand why it happens.

Sometimes, however, there can be legitimate reasons for interviewing people you know, for example if they are a victim or a witness in an event which you are covering. The listener does not need to be informed that they are known to you. The chances are that if you are a long-standing local radio reporter who knows the patch well and has lots of contacts, you will often come across people you have met before.

If the person you interview for your report or programme is the best choice to offer information to the listener, then they should be used. There is always the option of asking a colleague to conduct the interview if you feel it is inappropriate for you to be doing it, particularly if it is going to be a long and in-depth piece. Some reporters find it impossible to interview a relative or friend, because they cannot assume their professional mode with someone whom they usually relate to in a personal way.

INTERVIEWING WITH AN INTERPRETER

You have three things to record if you are planning to interview someone who does not speak the same language as you, or does not feel comfortable or confident enough to answer in another language. First record yourself asking the question, then record the interviewee's reply, followed by the translation spoken by the interpreter. It should not be necessary to record or use the question as asked by the interpreter. But it is important for mixing and editing purposes that you discuss with the interpreter how the interview should be conducted. In other words, request that the interpreter does not interrupt, make any interjections or deliver any reaction remarks during the reply, nor put any supplementary questions unless you have asked them first. Allow a pause between the interviewee's answer and the translation by the interpreter to ease the editing process. When you return to the studio, select the question-and-answer material that you want to use, and in the final mix of the interview allow the interviewee to begin replying in their own language before lowering the voice level and overlaying it with the translated reply given by the interpreter. A few words into the answer, you can fade out the interviewee, leaving just the voice of the interpreter. At the end of a translated answer you may want to bring up the voice of the interviewee again for the last couple of words of their original reply.

INTERVIEWING TECHNIQUES FOR DOCUMENTARIES

The secret of interviewing for documentaries is to take a few deep breaths before you even start thinking about recording anybody. The characteristics of a documentary include depth and detail in the coverage of the topic, an extended duration, first-hand experiences described by the contributors, and the exploitation of the medium of sound. These need to be borne in mind when you embark on the process of collecting interview material. Although you will devote a lot of time to individual interviews, it is important not to record too much material, especially if the time you have available for editing purposes is limited. You may also find that your contributor can only spare so much time to talk to you, so set the parameters before you start. Just as with any other form of programme format, your interviewees need to know the purpose and style of the finished product.

I find that it sometimes helps to stop recording after a few minutes to take a breather and allow the interviewee to relax. It is your job to give them a few words of encouragement at this stage – nothing over the top, simply 'That was very good, you're doing well.' When you start up again they often find it easier to talk. There can be a problem with continuity of thought when you record large amounts of material in one sitting. Your interviewee may think they have said something when in fact they haven't, and they quite often say things like 'as I said earlier', or 'as I was telling you before', which again can cause problems at the editing stage of the production. Contributions to a documentary need to be spoken with confidence and authority, so if you feel that the interview is not going as well as it should, then it is probably better to terminate it and start again. You can tell your interviewee that the recording was really just a rehearsal to check levels, acoustics, etc. Then go on to give some indirect advice on how they could improve their performance. For example, you could say 'What you said about the way that employees were treated at this time was very interesting, so we must get that part in. Perhaps it would be clearer for the listener if you start with that little anecdote before you explain what happened next. What do you think?' Radio news journalists are used to asking short and precise questions to get short and precise answers for use in their wraps or packages. Questioning for documentaries sometimes also calls for this style of approach, but more often it is a case of allowing the interviewee to open up slowly and gradually reveal their story. Sometimes just one well-worded open question will set them off on a train of thought and will produce some revealing material. If the interviewer is doing most of the talking, then something is going wrong. Documentaries should show rather than tell their story, with interviews from contributors providing the bulk of the information, and there should be less on-air material provided by the questions and links of the presenter.

Techniques like those used in montage production, which allow some of the interview material to stand alone or be juxtaposed with other interviewee clips, can be used to great effect in documentaries. You should also think about creating a picture in the mind of the listener by getting your interviewee involved in some kind of appropriate activity as they speak, for example if they are demonstrating how something works. Do not fall into the trap of doing all the talking yourself; be prepared to hand over control for a short time to allow the interviewee to describe the view or an object, or even commentate on an event. Record the sounds of the activity separately after the interview, to use in the mixing of the piece. You may want to use these sounds underneath some of your scripted links, or to fade in at the start or fade out at the end of the interview. Sounds can also be used to signify location or time. For example, the sound of an owl hooting will indicate nighttime in a lonely place, or the cawing of crows will give the impression of being in a graveyard during daytime. Sounds can also be used to indicate the passing of time by fading out one sound, pausing, then fading in another sound.

Incidentally, the use of sound effects which are available on pre-recorded disk or tape is not recommended. A listener is bound to notice that you have chosen birdsong which can only be heard in an obscure part of the country, or that the car noise was generated by an 1100cc engine and not a 1500. Be as honest with the sounds as you would be with the interview material.

INTERVIEWING FOR FEATURES

Like the documentary, a feature will often be broadcast as a stand-alone piece. Its production can use the simplest techniques of combining clips, links and actuality, or the more complicated use of montage, dramatic reconstruction or audio diary to tell its story. It is important to be aware of how interview material will be used in the finished feature before embarking on the interview process. Features will involve you spending more time in the preparation and production. Unlike a package, it will not necessarily conform to an accepted formula. The finished product will be longer and contain more elements. The format should allow you to explore ideas in more depth, and perhaps in a more iconoclastic way as creativity and imagination can come into play. The topic chosen for a feature should have something fresh or unusual to say about the subject by avoiding well-covered ground. Like documentaries, they could have a logical structure which may be provided by the story itself. For example, you may be preparing to tell the story of a day in the life of a game-keeper, or explaining the process of how a pint of milk reaches your doorstep, through a sequential order of events which can work very well on radio. It is worth considering using the strength of sound and acous-tics by recording interview or commentary material as you move from one room to another, from downstairs to upstairs, inside to outside, etc. Features can also benefit from the use of a core interviewee, who pro-vides the central linking thread throughout the piece and is supported by minor interviewee contributions. One of the more effective tech-niques that has been used in feature making involves combining inter-view material from the contributor with extracts from their own audio diary, which they have been left to record themselves after some train-ing in the use of the recorder and microphone.

INTERVIEWING FOR MONTAGES

Producing a montage can be a bit like a producing a sophisticated ver-sion of a vox-pop. However, the longer the montage, the more compli-cated it is to produce and the more challenging it is for the listener. Without the benefit of links from a presenter to guide them through the piece, it is up to the producer to signpost and label everything for the listener. This therefore places a further level of responsibility on the col-lection of the interview material at source and its editing, to assist in the eventual construction of the feature or documentary. The montage relies totally on the fruits of the interview. The answers of the contribu-tors can be mixed with other sounds, and perhaps most effectively with pauses, but the montage technique demands that the voice of the inter-viewer be lost completely. All the answers must stand alone or be juxta-posed one against another.

The quality of the background atmosphere must be either consistent or negligible, to allow for effective mixing.

INTERVIEWING FOR CLIPS

The interviewer should be listening out for soundbite opportunities – the short and concise answer containing a fact or two to establish the story, or an opinion giving a certain edge or a possible insight into how the story will move forward. Can you find the right question that will give you the answer you need? The answer that sums it all up in about twenty seconds and can be edited out cleanly? You may decide to ask just one question because you only need one answer as your clip. With developing news stories there is little time for planning or research, but try to go to an interview with a couple of relevant and informed questions at the ready. You could always suggest to your interviewee ways that they could encapsulate a long and detailed answer they have just given into a neat summary for you to record. If both of you are happy with the result, then why not? Experienced interviewees may also ask you how long an answer you need for your clip or wrap, etc., and be able to provide a tailor-made response on the spot. Interviewing simply to provide a clip for use in a news bulletin needs to be either a quickfire event or a careful choice from a longer piece. Quite often a clip will be taken from a recording off transmission (ROT) made of a live interview from earlier in a programme and included with some copy in a later bulletin. For example:

NEWSREADER   Midchurch Council meets tonight to discuss controversial plans to turn North Street into a traffic-free zone. Local shopkeepers who oppose the scheme say they will lobby councillors at the meeting. Bookshop owner Michael Green will be voicing the concerns of the North Street Traders Association.

MICHAEL GREEN   The Council needs to understand that local businesses are under a lot of pressure as it is without the chaos and confusion this scheme would cause. We don't think there has been enough consultation about the plans with the local shopkeepers or their customers. What we want is a chance to tell them what we think about it.

INTERVIEWING FOR WRAPS

The wrap involves a recorded voice report wrapped around a single clip of an interview answer. For example:

REPORTER   The accident happened in thick fog at about six o'clock this evening at the height of the rush hour. Traffic soon built up on the northbound carriageway, causing tailbacks of over two miles. Emergency services were quickly on the scene and diversions put into operation. Cab driver Frank Smith saw the coach swerve off the road into the field.

CAB DRIVER   The driver seemed to lose control and then the coach seemed to skid before it crashed into the fence. The next thing I saw it fall onto its side. It was lucky nobody was killed.

REPORTER   Passengers in the coach were taken to Midchurch General Hospital, but none are thought to be seriously injured.

The links would have been recorded by the reporter in the studio, and the cab driver's comments clipped from an interview recorded at the scene of the accident.

Think about how the surplus answers in the interview that you don't clip for use in the wrap could form the basis of information you can use in your links. Once again, another source of clips for use in your wrap could come from the recording of a live interview featured earlier in the programme. The wrap would usually feature just one voice clip together with links from the reporter.

INTERVIEWING FOR PACKAGES

Packages are halfway between a wrap and a feature. The success of the package relies not only on the interviewing skills of the reporter, but also their ability to tell a sometimes complex story in a straightforward and succinct way through sharp writing, ruthless editing and creative presentation. It is a technique that can also be used to liven up the telling of a story that is perhaps mundane or lacking in substance. The package will probably include two or more different voices. As the name suggests, the package should contain all you need to know about the latest development or viewpoints within a story, all neatly wrapped up in an attractive form.

The pace of the package is dependent on the duration and number of interview clips you include in the piece. A number of short interview clips will give a faster pace; a few longer clips a slower pace. The subject of the package should determine how the clips are used. The more serious subjects are likely to be more effective if clips are longer, and a light subject could benefit from short ones.

If time is against you it is possible to package on location, if you prepare the ground by writing the opening and closing links for your package and recording them on site, rather than waiting until you get back to the station. Studio time may be restricted, or you may be spending a greater part of your day travelling to and from the locations where your stories are based. I once had to cover two stories in a day from the same neck of the woods but quite a distance from the station. I also had a strict deadline to meet. One was a story about a new flat-bottomed boat that had been donated to a moated castle by a local organisation, and the other was the opening of a public exhibition of proposed routes for a village by-pass.

At the castle I climbed into the boat with one of the castle staff and a representative from the organisation that had donated the boat. I recorded the sound of the boat being rowed out on the moat for a few seconds, then recorded my opening link that explained that the boat was used to inspect the castle walls from the water and to rescue sheep that had strayed into the moat. I asked the boatman a couple of questions, then asked the donor a couple of questions. I recorded my closing link and a few more rowing noises. All of this without switching off the recorder. Once back at the station it would simply be a case of trimming to time the two short interviews in the middle of the recording, and topping and tailing the tape. But before returning to base it was off to the by-pass exhibition, where I recorded some traffic noise and my opening link, and faded out the traffic noise on my recorder using the recording level control. Inside the village hall I faded in the background hum of voices and recorded my second link, followed by a short interview with a person who was in favour of the route and another with a person who was against the route. I recorded another link, taped a short interview with an engineer from the highways department, then recorded a closing link.

To avoid fluctuations in levels it was necessary to keep input levels constant by pre-setting them and varying the position of the hand-held microphone. Back at the station it was only necessary to tidy up the interviews. In both cases the final editing work and cue writing was done in the newsroom, so no studio time was required for mixing them – I didn't have to join the queue of fraught reporters trying to get into the studio, and the editor had two simple packages for the drivetime programme.

Choosing music for use in package production is time-consuming and fraught with complications. For example, choosing a piece of music just because the title has something to do with the subject you are reporting is not advisable. I once heard a package about the changing role of nannies, in which the producer had incorporated the Rolling Stones' song 'Mother's Little Helper' – an inappropriate choice as the song is all about distraught mothers turning to tranquillisers for support. Perhaps it was meant to be an ironic choice, but I missed it at the time. A short extract from the title song to the science fiction film *Men in Black*, used in a package about the shortage of football referees, was quite a clever choice but it did grate a little, and distracted me, and others too I suspect, from hearing the piece properly.

The choice of a musical cliché can also grate on the listener. You might want to try and find something other than 'Food, Glorious Food' from the musical *Oliver* to accompany your links and clips in a report on school dinners; or 'Our House' by Madness in your piece about house prices – these have been used so many times before that they have lost their impact and novelty value. Remember your audience. Older listeners may not know the latest chart music, and younger listeners will be confused by some choices from past eras. Do not make assumptions. You may think using Handel's 'Water Music' is a good choice to use in your package about an increase in water rates, but the reference may be lost on some of your listeners.

ORAL HISTORY

The use of reminiscences and memories of a bygone age has been part of news features and documentaries for a long time, and tends to come in and out of favour with broadcasters. One year there are complaints of too much nostalgia, and the next year it is flavour of the month as an important anniversary is marked and radio journalists are sent far and wide across their patch to record the feelings and memories of the public. They will be listening out for good anecdotes, local angles and eye-witness accounts. I believe every radio station should have an archive of interview material; not only a collection of the best of the interviews heard live on air, but also interviews about specific subjects like working conditions, shopping facilities, housing, traditions, and so on. A lot of material comes from interviews with local characters and others with good memories for local history, and who may not be around for many more years, but oral history or the recalling of memories is not restricted to the elderly. Anyone can talk about their experiences, regardless of their age. Photographs and newspaper reports are available, but it would be a shame to lose forever the actual voices of local people talking in their own words about the world they know. These interviews provide a wealth of interesting and useful programme-making material for future reference, as well as providing a local and appropriate sound archive for the community which the station serves. Many people who are actively involved in the collection of oral history use it for social study purposes, and for this reason it is often deliberately archived unedited. The BBC has invested time and money in producing material for their *The Century Speaks* project, which puts the collection of oral history into the hands of broadcasters who have the extra task of converting 6,000 interviews into listenable programmes. Other programmes that have made use of this kind of interview material include *20th Century Vox* on Radio 5 Live, and *My Century* on BBC World Service.

Looking through your contacts book may not provide you with the source of potential interviewees. Your local library, museum, history group or organisations like the WI or WRVS may be a good starting point, and it may even be worth putting out an appeal during programmes on your own station and giving a phone number where people can contact you.

Collecting audio material of this kind demands a slightly different approach to interviewing than those adopted by most reporters, and can certainly be more time-consuming.

This is perhaps a more intimate form of interviewing which for the interviewee should not feel like an interview. The interview will often take place in the home of the interviewee. The contributor needs to be relaxed and unhurried. Try not to interrupt with questions, and let the contributor explain and describe things at their own pace.

The choice of microphone is important. Not just for technical quality, but to be as unintrusive as possible. The usual hand-held microphone can be indiscreet and draws attention to the fact that the conversation is being recorded, and it can be intimidating for the interviewee. For indoor interviews, small lapel microphones attached to the interviewee and yourself once you are sitting comfortably, are discreet enough to be eventually ignored. Be aware that this type of microphone is vulnerable to being struck by the interviewee, and needs to be unclipped before they can leave their seat. If possible, allow the interviewee to attach the microphone to themselves if they are able.

Keep your questions as open as possible and use everyday English. It is important that your interviewee feels that you are really interested in what they have to tell you, and that you are not just there to do a job. This will be shown in the way you ask questions. If you read every one from a prepared list it will be obvious you are not listening. Be aware that you may need to pause occasionally if the memories stir up emotional feelings in the interviewee, or if they are becoming tired. Be patient and sympathetic should these situations arise.

Unlike other interviews when you would usually rush off to get back to the studio to edit the piece for the deadline, you should take time to chat informally once the recording is over. Enjoy a cup of tea. Your contributor has worked hard for you and may even be feeling a little high or even a little sad after sharing memories which they haven't even thought about for years, let alone shared with a stranger, so continue with your polite and patient approach for a little longer.

INTERVIEWING ON MAGAZINE PROGRAMMES

Magazine programmes, which can last from half an hour to three hours, offer the opportunity to conduct interviews on a variety of subjects in both live and recorded formats. The material used in a news magazine programme is determined by the day's news agenda; a specialist programme will focus on its specific subject area, and programmes on local stations tend to approach all their topics from the 'how does it affect our listeners?' angle.

An interview-based programme like *Desert Island Discs* is recorded in advance of broadcast, and features a single notable interviewee in a gently paced, gently probing conversation about their life and times, interspersed with extracts of their favourite music which reflect their taste and illustrate their history. *Home Truths* features many interviewees, none of whom are celebrities, but who have a good yarn to tell. They are featured mostly pre-recorded down the line or on the phone, and in packages, etc., which include location interviews. They are structured with a mixture of live and recorded material to give variety and pace to the programme. The guests on *Midweek* are all in the studio together from start to finish of the programme, so that they can be interviewed individually and converse between themselves. In *Live From London* the interviewees not only face questions from an interviewer but have the extra anxiety of doing it in front of a theatre audience. To the listener, the studio-based interview programmes can offer a comfortable and pleasant environment for eavesdropping on conversations. Gentle lines of questioning are frequently adopted, and often the aim is to produce entertaining interviews. Sometimes these sorts of programmes can sound as if they are simply an opportunity to plug a guest's latest book, film, TV programme, theatre show, etc., and interviews with celebrities, particularly comedians, can sometimes result in the interviewer simply playing the part of a stooge and feeding leading questions that allow the guest to perform. If the programme is a long one, an interviewer may be forced to be over-indulgent, and interviews can go on for longer than they are worth. It is also important to remember that what may be fascinating to the interviewer may not be so for the listener. The interviewer may say 'we could talk about this all day', but could the audience listen to it all day?

AS-LIVE INTERVIEWS

Because of time constraints it may sometimes be necessary to pre-record an interview with a guest, but, in order to maintain the style of the programme, to introduce it to the listener as though it is being conducted live. This is a widely accepted presentation technique, and there is no suggestion that we are trying to cheat, fool or lie to the listener. Introducing a taped interview by saying that you 'spoke to so-and-so earlier' can take away that sense of now that is one of radio's strengths. Take as an example a daily magazine programme that features three separate short interviews during its first hour and one long interview during the second hour, all conducted by the presenter of the programme and positioned amongst music selections. The programme is designed to sound live and immediate and relies solely on the personality presenter and their interviewing skills, without any packaged stories or input from other interviewers. Arrangements have been made to interview the second-hour guest and two of the first-hour guests live in the studio. The third interviewee is going to be in a studio in another part of the country, or even abroad. Unfortunately it is not always possible to book the outside studio, or the connecting line or feed, for the time you need to conduct the interview live into the programme, so you arrange for the presenter to record the interview at a more convenient time before the programme goes out on air. The interview is recorded as if it is happening in real time. The cue and the opening question are edited out, so that the interview starts with the first answer provided by the interviewee. When it is time to broadcast the interview, the presenter will read the cue and ask the opening question as though the interviewee is at the other end of the line at that particular moment. The interview is then played out. The secret of success in playing in 'as-lives' lies in some subtle techniques:

- The interview should be recorded in the same studio from which the live programme will be broadcast, on the same day as the broadcast, and be conducted using the same microphone used by the presenter for the programme. This will help avoid noticeable changes in acoustic, tone or levels.

- The cue should be slightly ambiguous. By saying 'Joining me on the line from our Paris studio is Dr Martin Jones', or 'Dr Martin Jones knows all about this issue and is in our Paris studio', or 'Dr Martin Jones in our studio in Paris – what is the current state of play?' you are not stating that he is there at this moment.

- When you edit out the cue and first question, rather than cut tight up to your interviewee's first word, leave in the pause which will contain some line noise or studio atmosphere, so that the first answer will have a more natural feel when it is played in.

- If the interview has been conducted face-to-face in the studio earlier in the day, the presenter should go through the motions of reading out the cue, welcoming the guest and asking their first question in the same way, before the interview is played. The presenter should also open their guest's microphone and look up as if the guest were occupying the empty studio chair opposite. This will give the preamble a more natural-sounding presentation.

These techniques will help contribute to the acoustic and atmosphere of a live studio and help maintain the feel of immediacy.

RUNNING ORDER

The structure of a magazine programme, and the running order of the interviews featured in it, are important elements in the delivery of material to the listener. Interviews may need to be organised in such a way as to allow live guests to be ushered in and out of studios, to make contact with contributors down the line, and to establish phone links. Imagine you are producing a half-hour magazine programme about food which will contain six different interviews, as in the following list – in which order would you choose to place each interview, and what are the reasons for your choices? Consider that some of the interviews are live and others recorded. Do you choose the most topical and controversial to lead or end your programme? Should the recorded interviews be sandwiched between two live interviews at the start and finish, or should you alternate between live and recorded? Are there any natural links between one item or another that means they will sound right following one another? Which interview will grab your listeners' attention and convince them to stay listening throughout the whole programme?

1   A live studio interview with a government minister on the subject of the latest food scare. Approximately four minutes in duration.

2   A recorded interview, illustrated with music extracts, with a popular songwriter about how food is celebrated through song. Approximately four minutes in duration and one of a regular series of interviews with well-known personalities about food and the arts.

3   Recorded interviews with a group of students living away from home, on their eating habits. Duration approximately three minutes.

4   Live discussion about choosing foods that will help relieve the symptoms of stress. Two interviewees; one in the studio, the other down the line from her health clinic. Duration approximately five minutes.

5   A recorded package featuring interviews with managers of restaurants, supermarkets, support agencies and charities, about a plan to distribute surplus food to those in need in the UK. Duration approximately six minutes.

6   Live studio interview with a historian on food fads down the ages. This week the 1920s. Approximately five minutes in duration.

I would suggest that there is no perfectly right or completely wrong answer to the choices you make. However, some suggestions will be more appropriate than others.

A programme may feature just one guest who will be interviewed in some depth. These interviews can range from the sort featured in *Analysis*, on BBC Radio 4, which had a reputation for in-depth, probing, analytical and intellectually challenging interviewing, through to a veteran thespian being interviewed about their career on a local radio chat show. Whatever the subject or interviewee, the principles of preparation should be the same. A longer interview demands more careful research, attention to detail and profile information. From the interviewer's point of view it can be a challenging event as they try to keep the interview focused yet stimulating, and their concentration and listening capabilities sharp. Knowing the profile of the listener is also important if the interview is to be pitched correctly, and assumptions should not be made that everyone listening will have the same awareness or previously accumulated knowledge of the topic or person being featured. The interviewer's introductory cue must be designed not only to stimulate an interest in the forthcoming interview, but to summarise and provide information that will enable everyone to listen from the same starting point. For example, I have read all the novels of author Iain Banks, and have heard, read and watched interviews with him about his work, but I would not expect everyone else who is about to listen to an interview with him to be the same as me, so I would expect the interviewer to take a little time to at least acquaint others with a background summary, or to feature an extract or reviews from one of his books.

INTERVIEWING PHONE-IN CALLERS

Public contributions into radio programmes via their home telephones began in 1968, when the BBC's local radio station in Nottingham set the ball rolling. Today there are few stations that do not have some form of interaction with their listeners via the phone. These include competitions, advice lines to the expert in the studio, discussion and debate, and on some stations traffic jambusters, who call from their car phones or mobiles when they are stuck in traffic to warn listeners of potential delays.

Problems can arise if the quantity or quality of callers is inconsistent. To encourage callers, the topics for discussion should be stimulating and broad enough to have wide appeal; your studio guest should be knowledgeable and amiable; and your presenter/interviewer authoritative and impartial. In *Call Nick Ross* on BBC Radio 4, people with experience or specific knowledge about the topic of the day were invited to call in, and Brian Hayes on BBC Radio 2 would insist that you called in to his programme only if you could add something to the debate and were prepared to have your views and opinions challenged.

Telephone line quality is usually acceptable for short live or recorded interviews or an answer for a clip or wrap, if the contributor is unable to get into main or satellite studios for a line interview. Using the telephone for longer interviews is usually discouraged, but if no other method is available it can be a lifeline, even with poor, but acceptable technical quality. Conducting an interview with someone on a mobile phone is still a risky business.

Do not underestimate the importance of the off-air phone interview that takes place prior to broadcast and is conducted by the person or team answering the calls. It is not just a case of picking up the phone, giving the name of the programme and getting the caller's name. It is essential that some initial sorting and selecting of callers is done at this stage. The person answering should be trained and experienced enough to ask the caller some questions to establish what it is they are likely to say or argue. This will then enable the producer or presenter to choose a variety of views and callers to give the phone-in balance and structure. It may also be necessary to weed out callers who offer potentially unhelpful contributions. Presenters of phone-ins also like to know what a caller is likely to say so that they can prepare follow-up questions to the contribution – questions like 'Why do you feel that?', 'Are your opinions based on personal experiences?', and so on. Knowing a little of the caller's background can help the presenter to perhaps shorten the story the caller is going to tell and give them more time to explain the reasons behind their opinions, feelings or attitude. Some callers end up spending a lot of air-time describing the fine details of their case or situation. To avoid this the presenter can outline this information in their cue into the caller: 'Our next caller is Mary. Mary, your daughter suffered at the hands of bullies at school. Is that why you would like to see these changes introduced?' By first outlining the caller's story, you can get down to the nitty-gritty and give them more time to express and explain their point of view.

Interviewing someone on the phone during a programme can be a more relaxed experience for some interviewees who are used to talking on the phone, but the interviewer is unable to give the usual visible encouragement to the interviewee and is often tempted to fall back on the verbal encouragement of 'I see', 'Yes, I understand', and even 'Uh-huh', which they normally avoid.

Some phone interviewees may not be aware they are on air and that they are taking part in a preliminary research chat and providing background information. It is important that they are made aware that they are being interviewed for broadcast.

Callers can be lost between the room where the calls are received and the studio presenter, resulting in dead air and time wasted asking 'Mrs Smith, are you there?' or 'Can you hear me, Mr Jones?' from whoever is fronting the interview. If this happens to you, then give up on the call and say something like 'We seem to have lost contact with Mrs Smith. I hope we can talk to her a little later. In the meantime … '.

If your interviewee is speaking from a public call box, call them back. This means the station pays for the call and you will not suddenly hear the pips over the air, and the caller will not be cut off in their prime because their money has run out. Stories abound on every station about how reporters have tried to conduct interviews on the phone, only to have the conversation interrupted by the caller's dog barking, the doorbell ringing, babies crying, or someone talking on an extension.

If you are interviewing callers during a phone-in programme, resist the temptation to 'squeeze in one final quick caller' before the end of the programme. The conversation could sound rushed or the caller might be very long-winded and the programme will end scrappily. Best to finish with a summary, or to thank the callers and apologise to those whom you did not have time to hear from during the show.

INTERVIEWING VIA A SATELLITE OR REMOTE STUDIO

These small studios are very useful when a contributor is unable to travel to the main studio for a face-to-face interview. There are now plenty of them dotted around, and it is almost possible to link to anywhere in the country. From the listener's point of view the technical quality is such that interviewer and interviewee sound as if they are sitting next to each other.

There are distinct disadvantages from the interviewer's point of view. Like the telephone interview, you cannot see your opposite number, so you are unable to nod or smile encouragement. Neither can you observe their body language or see if they are reading from notes.

If you are conducting an interview with two participants, one next to you in the studio and the other from another studio, the person speaking down the line can sometimes feel as though they are playing second fiddle; they can feel excluded from the activity in the main studio, and may also be unsure about whether they can interrupt or interject during the debate.

There is also the risk of interruptions by someone entering the room, or someone disconnecting the link between the two studios. At an unmanned studio the interviewee is expected to set up the equipment themselves, so they may make mistakes. Problems can arise when a contributor cannot find the light switch or the main power switch, or when they put the telephone down even when they are told not to. And at the end of the interview, in their rush to get away they may forget to switch off the studio equipment.

INTERVIEWING VIA RADIO CAR

Most radio stations use a radio car for broadcasting live interviews from a location or complete outside-broadcast programmes, and for providing a live link with a contributor, either an interviewee or a correspondent/ reporter on location. The car is usually painted up with the station's name and reception frequency which it advertises as it moves from one location to another around the patch. It is important that the car is driven courteously and carefully, as it is part of the public image of the station. The most noticeable feature of the radio car is the mast transmitter which sticks out of the roof of the car; it is distended when the car is being driven and can be extended into the air to send the signal back to the studio for live broadcast or recording the material back at base. The radio car also has the facility to send a recorded piece to air using a portable tape recorder. For example, you may arrive at a site to conduct a live interview but be unable to get the car and hence the microphone close enough to the action, and the action cannot come to the car. There may also be times when the signal from the site is not strong enough for broadcast purposes. In this case you will record the interview at the site on a portable recorder, remembering that you will not be editing the piece; then you can plug it into the car and play it in when required. Make sure there is plenty of charge in the tape recorder's batteries or the tape will run slow or stop altogether during playback. If the signal you send from the car is not powerful enough, drive it to a new location – higher ground usually works – and play in your taped interview from there.

CHAIRING THE DISCUSSION OR DEBATE

If you invite a number of interviewees to take part in a round-table discussion, as well as trying to get answers to questions you may find yourself having to chair the debate. This can mean ensuring that all the guests get an equal opportunity to speak and that the debate is handled in a fair and impartial way.

When you book guests for a discussion, make sure that everyone is fully briefed about what the discussion is to be about, who will be taking part and what views they represent. Don't try and hide anything in the hope that it will enliven the interview when information is revealed on air. Chances are someone will cry foul, and your reputation and standing will take a beating. It's best to leave the guests to initiate anything controversial.

In the interest of good listening there is always the temptation, which should be avoided, to concentrate on interviewing the best performer – the one who stays calm and collected, who seems to be sensible and reasonable, who answers succinctly and knowledgeably.

If one of your guests has a habit of giving rambling answers, try breaking in at an appropriate point by saying 'That's an interesting point you make', or 'You mentioned that … ', and then turn to another guest and say 'What do you think about this?' or 'How do you respond to that point?' This should re-establish your control over the discussion, achieve a polite interruption, refocus the conversation away from the rambling guest, and move the debate on.

The same technique of interrupting dominant speakers could also be adapted and used to encourage less vocal contributors to participate more.

Someone will always want the last word. After all, they will be leaving a final thought in the mind of the listener. In the interests of balance, fairness and diplomacy it may be a good idea to leave a few seconds for the interviewer to round things off and end the discussion smoothly.

When you are in the chair, use the same techniques that you use when interviewing. Indicate positively who you want to speak next in the discussion; show an interest and encourage those speaking by nods, etc.; have notes about the questions you want to ask; avoid allowing two people to speak at once; keep an eye on the clock; and wind up proceedings so that they finish tidily.

VOX-POP INTERVIEWS

Some interviewers love recording vox-pops, others hate them. To be a successful vox-popper you need the thick skin of a market researcher and the tenacity of a door-to-door salesman. Like a market researcher canvassing the views of the public you must be prepared for some people to ignore you, avoid you or be abusive. Stopping people at random in the street and asking their views or opinions is hard work for such a short piece of air-time. Subjects like 'The existence of God' do not make good street-corner conversation, but those such as 'Sunday shopping laws' do. Gathering early opinions on a breaking news story can be a problem, as people may not have heard the story or not have had sufficient time to form opinions or even reactions. Remember, a vox-pop is an illustrative snapshot, not a definitive survey, and is best used to add texture to a piece or a programme – not used as the reason for featuring the subject under discussion. If you are working as a freelance, vox-pops can be financially devastating, because unless you have a system to produce a quick turnaround of the material, they will take up too much of your time, and if you are being paid for what goes out on air they will leave you bankrupt. Some further points:

- Try and persuade the editor who asks for a vox-pop to give you another longer interview or package that you can record in the same location at the same time.

- Decide on the exact wording of the question you intend to ask. It must be an open question – the last thing you want is a series of yes-or-no answers.

- Pick your location carefully – a pub may seem a good idea, but remember you may only get slurred speech, shouting and a lot of background noise. Pedestrian precincts and markets can be worthwhile, but stay outside unless you want muzak and public address announcements to ruin your recording. Stay away from pedestrian crossing points that have 'bleeping' signals – you can guarantee they will begin to make a noise during your recording, and you will find it difficult to remove them. In fact, try to avoid any location where the background noise is likely to be intermittent and will make your edits sound very obvious, because you will not be only editing the interview but the background noise at the same time; you cannot edit them separately.

- Try not to record your interviews in a variety of locations. Background noises may be different at each place, which will be noticeable when you come to link the clips together.

- Try and choose a location which is appropriate to the subject you are asking about, for example if you want to know about reading habits then talk to people leaving a local library or bookshop. At least you are more likely to get a recording because people will be in tune with the topic and ready to talk to you. What you don't want is a place that is too quiet or lacking in character, otherwise you may just as well arrange to conduct the interviews in the studio.

- Decide how you are going to approach your 'victim'. It is perhaps not a good idea to simply shove the microphone into their face and ask your question. Keep the microphone by your side as you approach. Your opening gambit needs to be short and simple, e.g. 'Hello I'm from Radio FM – can I talk to you about/ask your opinion about/ask you what you think about … '. Once you get the OK, bring the microphone up and ask your question.

- Put your recorder into record mode and use the pause button to save time and speed up the recording process. This technique is also useful to stop the recording of bores who go on and on. You will also be cutting out your voice in the final piece, so start the recording after you have asked the question to save time later.

- Edit and order the material in your head as you collect the vox-pops.

- Try for plenty of variety in the range of voices you collect – male and female, young and old. Remember, if you choose to vox-pop in a shopping precinct at ten o'clock in the morning you will most likely find yourself talking to shoppers, shopkeepers and visitors to the

area. Be prepared to be flexible about the time and venue for your
interviewing.

- Hope and strive for a wide range of opinions, and in the final edited
  piece arrange the pros and cons so that the views expressed present a
  good mix and are fairly evenly balanced.

- Remember to record some of the background noise from the location to run underneath the voices you have collected. This will give
  the piece a sense of place, and possibly help disguise any untidy
  edits.

- Only use answers that can be understood at first hearing, but do not
  reject any giggles or humorous replies that could be included.

- Vary the duration of answers you use to give the piece an interesting
  pace.

- Experiment with the juxtapositioning of the answers to give the
  vox-pop structure and body. Try to kick it off with a well-expressed
  and strongly felt opinion, and perhaps end on a lighter note.

- Just because you have used a voice once in the vox-pop does not
  mean you cannot use it again later in the same piece. I once used
  three clips from the same chap because he had a lot to say, was naturally funny and had a distinctive voice: I decided to exploit him for
  all he was worth.

A collection of answers to an open and very general question like 'What
do think about the proposals to ban traffic from North Street?' put to a
range of people could run like this in the final straightforward vox-pop:

[*Fade in traffic noise*]

Vox 1   I think it's a good idea. It'll certainly be a bit less noisy than it
is now.

Vox 2   Well, it would make it a bit safer for the old people and mothers
with kids. I'm surprised there haven't been any serious accidents
before now.

Vox 3   Dreadful idea. It'll kill off the trade if people can't drive up the
street. And what about the vans that deliver to the shops along
here?

Vox 4   There's been traffic coming along this street since the nine-
teenth century. If they stop it now it'll ruin the character of the
place.

Vox 5   I think they should ban traffic from the whole of the town centre, but it doesn't matter what I say, they'll do want they want anyway, won't they? (laughs)

[Fade out traffic noise]

8
After the interview

Once the interview is in the can there is still work to be done.

If it has been a live contribution in a studio, it should simply mean showing your guest to the door, thanking them and waving goodbye. Do make sure, however, that you have a contact number and address should you need to speak to them again. If it has been an interview about, say, a support group or event, you may get phone queries from listeners after the broadcast, so get a number or address where they can contact the organisation for further information or clarification of details.

If it was a studio recording of an interview for future broadcast, you need to start thinking about editing the tape and writing the cue sheet before the broadcast deadline, which may be minutes or days away.

RETAKES

If during the course of recording the interview you or your contributor are not happy with a particular answer, you have the option to stop, pause and retake the question-and-answer again. Retakes are best done at this stage to keep the pace and flow of the interview. Try to reassure your interviewee that the reason you need to retake is not because of their incompetence or mistakes.

If you decide at the end of the interview to retake any part of it, bear in mind that your contributor's voice and indeed yours may have changed in volume, tone or speed; that the position of the participants at the microphone may be slightly different; or that your contributor may have now relaxed and approach your retaken questions with a different attitude. Furthermore, any retakes will have to be edited into the piece, and could sound out of place and make the listener aware of the edit. The fact that the interview was conducted in a studio helps in that the background ambience should at least be consistent.

PLAYING BACK

Before your interviewee leaves the premises or you leave theirs, it is essential that you check that the interview has been recorded. If it has not, or there is another fault that causes it to be unusable, then you have no alternative but to apologise and do it again. You should really only need to check the final minute or two. Resist the temptation to play it all back at this stage, because your interviewee may not like what they hear and want to do it all, or even worse, parts of it, again.

Before you sit down to edit the interview, listen to the whole thing and make notes of what you need to remove.

EDITING

If you have recorded an interview on tape, cassette or disk, you will more than likely need to edit it before it is either broadcast or used as part of another longer recorded piece like a package or feature. Recorded interviews are edited:

- To remove mistakes and unwanted material.

- To change the duration of the interview by editing out or editing in material.

- To change the order of the material by transposing parts. Your first answer may end up sounding better at the end of the interview.

- To creatively exploit the material, perhaps in package or documentary production.

It wasn't until the 1950s and the invention of plastic magnetic tape for recording audio that quick and accurate editing became possible. There are now four methods of editing:

- Digital editing. This is a non-destructive form of sound editing. It is so called because you do not work on the original recording, but on a copy of it. The interview is downloaded into a computer which has a sound-editing software package installed. This has to be done in real time, so be selective about the material you put into the computer for editing. It is more efficient than just playing in all your recording, and means you will be working with material you want to use, not spending time removing material you did not want to keep in the first place. A visual representation of the sound appears on the screen in the form of a wave pattern, and you can listen to the actual sound via headphones or loudspeaker. Using the mouse to position a cursor on the screen, you can delete unwanted segments, or re-order material by repositioning it. The joy of this system is that you can undo any of your edits if you are not satisfied with the result. There is a temptation to spend all your time watching the screen, but keep reminding yourself that you are editing audio, something the listener only hears, and take time to look away from the screen and simply listen to the piece. The finished edit is either broadcast directly from the computer if it is linked to the studio, or dubbed onto tape, cart or minidisk and taken to the studio to be played out on air. This dubbing, like the downloading, has to be carried out in real time.

- Analogue or splice editing. This process involves marking the point of edit with a chinagraph (waxed) pencil, cutting the recorded tape with a one-sided blade, removing the unwanted material and joining the tape back together again with splicing tape. If your original interview has been recorded on open-reel tape then you will not need to dub the material but can begin editing, and once you have finished, can play it straight out on air. If you change your mind about an edit it means you must unpick the splicing tape and replace the original piece of tape you removed before you can proceed. This can be a problem if you have dropped the edited tape on the floor with the rest of the offcuts.

- Dubbing. Cutting cassette tape is not recommended. If you want to edit a recording made on a cassette player you need to dub or transfer the material to open-reel tape for splice editing, or to the computer for digital editing. Do not dub the entire recording – be selective and choose only the parts you are thinking of broadcasting. You can also simply transfer a clip from an interview on cassette onto a cart for broadcast if it does not require any tidying up. This applies to ordinary cassettes, DAT and minidisk.

- Shuffling. This is the term used when referring to the editing of material on a minidisk recorder, which can enable the user to re-order the material on disk or erase any parts not required. It is not editing in the true sense, perhaps, but more a shifting of material into preferred order, or erasing of it. But it is very useful, because it enables the interviewer to begin the process of rough editing material before they return to the studio to load it onto the computer or to dub it onto tape for actual cutting. This can save a lot of time.

Whatever system you use to edit your interview, there are the same editorial considerations:

- Your interviewee should be told that the interview will be edited before it is broadcast.

- To the listener, the end result should sound as though it has not been edited at all.

- The interview should be edited fairly so that the sense and spirit of what was said is still intact.

- The speech rhythm of the original recording should be maintained.

You also need to develop your own system and routines:

- Be aware of your broadcast deadline and keep an eye on the clock. Your edit decisions may be governed by the restrictions both of deadline and time-slot duration.

- To make life easy, an edit is usually made from the beginning of a sentence, preferably on the pause before the speech begins. If you find it necessary to edit mid-sentence, try to find a word that starts with a positive, clear sound like a letter B, P or S. These sounds can also be useful if you find yourself having to edit mid-word and join the first half of a word with the second part of another.

- Be aware that people breathe. If you edit out the breaths their words will be too close together to sound like natural speech patterns. However, breaths from discarded extracts of the interview can be useful to include in your piece at a point where you have made an edit but it does not sound natural.

- What if your interviewee has a stammer – should you try to remove it from their answer? The answer is basically no, but a little tidying up would be acceptable. However, if the piece is about stammering, then leave it as it is. The same goes for someone who says 'um' or 'er' or 'you know' frequently. Your interviewee or anyone who knows them will hear the difference, so you should not change the character of the person you are editing.

- Editing the interview can be a problem if the background noise is high. You may find that the speech part flows and sounds natural, but the changes in background, like the roar of traffic or music, give the edits away. If you find yourself in this position, you can try making your edit-point close to the first words of a new sentence or on a loud background sound. If this does not work, hunt around for another place to edit.

- Take time to listen through all your recorded material before you start deciding what to keep and what to discard. Rough edit the piece before you begin to fine edit. Start by selecting the parts of the interview you want to keep, rather than just removing the parts you do not want to use. The discarded parts may provide useful material to help you write your cue and links. Keep reminding yourself of the reason why you are editing the piece – is it simply to tidy it up, or is it to make it fit into a time slot, or is it to creatively shape the material? If you do not keep focused on the task it will affect the final outcome.

To be a good editor, whichever system of editing you use, you need to be fast and accurate. Once you have been shown how to do it, practise your skills as often as you can, as this is the only way to become more proficient.

CHOOSING CLIPS

- Remind yourself of the purpose of the interview.
- Think about the message your interviewee was trying to put across.
- The structure of your finished interview should answer the questions who, what, when, etc., in the most appropriate order.

- What are the little gems that shine out from the interviewee's contribution?

- Which parts of the interview could be summarised more succinctly in your script?

- Which material will be useful to include in the cue or back announcement?

- What time restraints apply – have you been asked to provide a forty-second clip, or several clips for a longer piece?

ADMINISTRATION

- Remember to add the full details of your interviewee and new contact in your contacts book for future reference.

- If you have arranged to notify the interviewee when the interview is to be broadcast, remember to give them a call. Point out that the interview is scheduled for a particular programme, date and time, but remind them that anything could happen and the piece could be re-scheduled by the producer/editor.

- You may have to complete a music log, with details of the duration of the music used and other label information, if you have used extracts from any commercial recordings.

- You may need to fill out an 'election log' if the interview is with a politician or party worker and is to be featured during the pending period of an election.

WRITING A CUE FOR THE INTERVIEW

A cue is the written introduction to a live or recorded interview, read by the person presenting the interview on air. It should be an informative but imaginative introduction to the topic and the interviewee. It is the *hors d'oeuvre* before the main course and should act as a taster for the listener. The idea of the cue is to grab the interest of the listener and make them want to hear more. It should also feature the important information that will enable them to understand the interview, for example the background to the story, the name and title of the interviewee, etc. Be guided by the radio station's house style for style and duration. Some stations do not offer any guidelines, but others may, for example, only allow three lines for the cue and not require an outcue. It is worth reminding yourself that the cue, particularly one that introduces a live contribution into a programme, may also subtly indicate to the listener how you think they should receive what is being said by your guest. The cue may also make assumptions about the character of your contributor or the subject under discussion, which again will influence how they are received by the listener. If your introduction is interpreted as disapproval, you could unintentionally be encouraging the listener to 'boo' the guest, as an audience at a pantomime greets the appearance of the villain.

Do not start writing the cue sheet until after you have finished editing the interview.

Do not leave it until the last minute. Allow time to complete it, because your cue needs to be thought about, and a couple of attempts may be needed to get it just right.

WRITING FOR THE EAR

- You have very little time, so what you say has to be carefully selected.

- You have no pictures, only words, so you have to create pictures in the mind of the listener. So use descriptive expressions like 'the size of a football pitch', rather than giving dimensions. Round up complicated numbers: 1,920 is easier to picture if you say 'nearly two thousand'.

- The listener, unlike the reader, only has one chance to take in what they hear.

- Deal with one topic at a time, don't jump about.

- Keep it simple. It is better to put across one or two ideas clearly than to try to include more and confuse the listener.

- Feed information in the order in which questions will arise in the mind.

- Lead from the general to the particular.

- Put the most important and the latest information first.

- Your words should give explanation, background, context and analysis.

- Answer the questions who, what, when, why, where and how in the order most appropriate to the story.

- Don't write your story, tell it. Speak the words aloud first before you write them. After all, you are writing them to be spoken aloud. If they sound right put them on paper.

- Write words as they will be spoken, e.g. didn't, hasn't. Radio English is spoken English, and even contains sentences that do not include verbs, e.g. 'Finally, tonight's main news headlines again' and 'This report from our education correspondent'.

- Start with a short sentence to grab the listener's attention. Remember, people communicate in short bunches of words.

- Avoid ambiguous expressions or complicated sentences, otherwise you will lose the listener's attention as they try to work out what has just been said.

- Broadcast English favours the present tense, even when referring to something in the future, e.g. 'On Radio 4 at seven fifteen Francine Stock takes her regular look at the arts in *Front Row*. In tonight's edition she meets the actor and author who ... '.

- Rely more on nouns and present active verbs. Use adjectives and adverbs sparingly to avoid flowery-sounding descriptions. There is no room in your script for wasted or decorative words.

- Use reported speech – there are no quotation marks on radio. For example, 'The minister said that his department would take immediate action to ease the problem', and not 'The minister said "My department will take immediate action to ease the problem."'

- Avoid lists.

- Explain any acronyms and technical terms you use, unless they are in regular use and well known to the general public.

- Check that names, facts and figures are all correct.

WRITING A CUE SHEET

Here is an example of a cue sheet to introduce a recorded interview. It shows the name of the reporter, the title of the piece, etc.

The cue itself should be concise, and printed on one side of the page only, in double spacing in sufficiently large type to make it easy for the presenter to read. Do not split a sentence or paragraph at the bottom of the page, otherwise the reader will have to turn to the next page as they are speaking.

Cues should not duplicate what the speaker is about to say. For example, in the example below, the last line of the cue would need to be changed if the opening lines of the first speaker were 'A new form of birth control may hold the answer … '.

At the top of the cue sheet is the name of the reporter and contributor, the slug and the date. After the introduction (cue) it contains useful information about the opening or 'in' words and the closing or 'out' words of the recorded piece and the total running time. A short 'back announcement' for the presenter to read rounds it all off.

Rachel Jones/Tim Smith Elephants 19 Sept. 2000 17.59

CUE

The large numbers of elephants now roaming an African wildlife park are causing problems for people living in nearby villages.

Houses are being damaged and crops destroyed, forcing the human population of Arusha in Tanzania to leave their homes and farms.

Conservationists say that the breeding programme designed to increase the once-dwindling elephant population has been too successful.

But as veterinary surgeon Rachel Jones, who works in the wildlife park, explains to our reporter Tim Smith, a new form of birth control may hold the answer.

IN: (FX elephant noises) The African elephant is one of …
OUT: … before it is too late. (FX rifle shots)
DUR: 3'38"

BACK ANNO.

Vet Rachel Jones talking to our reporter Tim Smith in East Africa, where elephants may soon be put on the pill.

The cue sheet is also a useful document for the person introducing the piece on air. Make sure adequate information has been provided to make their job easy. As well as the details mentioned in the example above, you may want to include an alternative 'out' where the duration is shorter, just in case the restraints of time mean that the piece as whole cannot be featured. This is useful in that it leaves the decision about where to stop the piece in your hands – after all, you know it better than anyone else – rather than leaving it to the presenter to make an arbitrary decision. If the piece ends with music or atmosphere, it is useful for the presenter to be told via the cue sheet whether the music fades, so that they can perhaps read the back announcement over it, or gain a few seconds by fading it early if they need to make up time.

PRESENTATION

You may be required to read a cue introducing your own or others' interviews. This is an important part of selling the interview to the listener, so do not put them off by throwing away the delivery. This advice is also applicable if you are expected to link your interview material in a recorded package, feature or wrap. Even if you are simply conducting an interview, do not assume your voice will sound perfect as soon as you open your mouth. Unfortunately, the microphone can highlight any weaknesses or faults in your presentation. Prepare yourself well for any voicework:

- Warm up the voice – practice tongue-twisters, recite poems, sing a verse of a song and clear the vocal passages.

- Encourage flexibility in your lips by either whistling a tune or trying a tongue-twister that uses lots of 'p' or 'b' sounds. For example: 'Peter Piper picked a peck of pickled peppers. If Peter Piper picked a peck of pickled peppers, where's the peck of pickled peppers Peter Piper picked?' Or try 'Betty beat a bit of butter and made a better batter.'

- Read and digest the information first, then use the script as an *aide-mémoire*. If you do not understand what you are reading, then the listener will also have difficulty grasping the plot. To check your understanding before you go on air, try reading the script aloud, then turn over the page and tell the story to yourself in your own words.

- Make your reading of any cues precise, authoritative and attention-grabbing through your speed of delivery and the tone in which you present the piece. Attack the script with relish, but try to sound relaxed.

- Try to read in a simple conversational style. Do not mumble. Do not swallow your words. Watch out for words that begin with p or b – if you are too close to the microphone they will cause popping.

- Aim to speak as if to one person.

- If you find yourself stumbling or fluffing, you may be speaking too quickly. Slow down your reading and you should regain the flow. If you do make a mistake, do not draw attention to it by apologising, blaming others or swearing – simply correct it and carry on. Other causes of fluffing on air are inadequate preparation, messy alterations to the text and distractions in the studio. Do whatever is necessary to avoid these problems.

- In the studio sit comfortably, directly facing the microphone. To allow your lungs, diaphragm and throat to do their job you should keep your airways unrestricted, so keep your head up, feet flat on the floor, back straight, shoulders relaxed, and loosen your collar.

  - Remove anything that may rattle or knock against the table (bracelets, watch, etc.). Switch off anything that contains an alarm facility (watch, phone, pager) or leave it outside the studio.

  - Check your headphones for comfort and volume.

  - Check the clock is correct.

  - Check your voice level.

COMMON PROBLEMS

There will always be the occasional word that will cause you problems. For a long time I avoided the word 'celebrity' because I always stumbled over it, and I knew that I would be concentrating so hard on getting it right that I would end up stumbling over other words that did not usually cause me any problems. It helps to practise the word you find difficult, but include a word or two before and after the problem word, so that you do not put too much emphasis on it.

You may notice some of your interviewees turning statements into questions by adopting a rising cadence at the end of their sentences. For example, 'I went to the shop at the end of the street' becomes 'I went to the shop at the end of the street?' This can be irritating and makes editing sentences more difficult. Avoid using this technique in your cues or scripts.

Many people have difficulty with words that begin with the 'th' sound, like 'think' which can come out as 'fink'. Reciting the following phrase may help: 'I sit and think and fish, I fish and sit and think, I think and sit and fish.'

Some people produce faulty 'r' sounds so that the word 'rock' sounds like 'wock'. How does the following sound when you say it: 'Round and round the ragged rock the ragged rascal ran.'

If you think that, like plenty of others, you produce a faulty 's' sound, then listen carefully when you say this line: 'Sing a song of sixpence.'

If you have a tendency to cut off the 'ing' endings of words like 'singing', then practise this little gem: 'Grab a gloriously gleaming green glass.'

VOCABULARY

As *Readers Digest* always says, 'It pays to increase your word power.' Every journalist should love language and develop their range of vocabulary, but because radio is about writing for the spoken word, it is important that broadcasters should not lose touch with new words and expressions, and at the same time not become alienated from the listener by using words not in common parlance, words that are too trendy or too highbrow. I am not advocating 'dumbing down' because the listener is ignorant, or saying that the average listener is incapable of thought or of enjoying thought-provoking discussion. Words need to be clearly understood, otherwise the broadcaster does not communicate to the listener. Language develops and changes, but the journalist should retain a respect for the language and be careful to avoid abusing or misusing it. You cannot stop an interviewee using shoddy speech, but the listener will expect you to use language clearly and accurately, even if you are trying to be concise. Words should be chosen carefully, be precise, consistent and non-adjectival, and should avoid subjective judgement. Our writing needs to be clear and easily understood because, unlike when reading a newspaper, our listener cannot rewind a broadcast and listen to something again.

CLICHÉS

Journalists should never be at a loss for words, but a convenient or neat turn of phrase can become over-used. Expressions like 'sick as a parrot', 'at the end of the day', 'at this moment in time' and 'the offer on the table', do not appear as often as they used to, probably because so many jokes have been made at the expense of those who use such expressions. Here are a few that are still heard regularly on air:

A question mark hangs over ...

Dawn revealed the true horror ...

New look ...

The campaign got under way ...

A report out today ...

Services ground to a halt ...

A full-scale manhunt is under way ...

A new deal is in the pipeline.

GRAMMAR

The over-emphasis of 'The' and 'A' at the beginning of sentences for extra impact is a source of irritation for some listeners and can elicit accusations of sloppy speech. So it is preferable to hear from 'The Prime Minister ... ' and not from 'Thee Prime Minister ... ', and to hear about 'A [as in cat] new law banning smoking ... ', not 'A [as in cake] new law banning smoking ... '.

Unlike newspapers, the titles Mrs, Ms or Mr before someone's name are not used in radio, so Mr Tom Smith or Mr T. Smith is always 'Tom Smith' when the name is first mentioned, but 'Mr Smith' may be used for later references in the story or script.

PRONUNCIATION

Radio journalists do not necessarily have to spell names correctly, but they have to pronounce them correctly. Always get your interviewee to say their name on tape if it is an unusual one. This way you can hear how it should be pronounced.

Unless you want calls and letters from irate listeners, make sure you pronounce any place names correctly.

American pronunciation often slips into everyday conversation. The following words are often incorrectly pronounced. This is not an exhaustive list by any means.

vite-a-min	instead of vitamin
comparable	stress on first syllable
controversy	stress on first syllable
plice	instead of police
drawring	instead of draw-ing
secerterry	instead of secretary
says	instead of sez
Febuary	instead of February (Feb-roor-i)
joolery	instead of jewellery (jewel-ry)
vunnerable	instead of vulnerable
burgalry	instead of burglary
nucular	instead of nuclear (new-cleer)
registary	instead of register office

ACCURACY

It may be stating the obvious, but nothing broadcast by a radio station, including interviews, should contain racist, sexist, homophobic or misogynist references or material. It is also quite easy to be inadvertently ageist or sizeist. Any form of labelling should be avoided as it can arouse strong feelings.

Is it 'Chairman', 'Chairwoman', 'Chairperson' or 'Chair'? Perhaps it is whatever the person heading the committee chooses themselves to refer to their position.

'Fire-fighters' should be used in place of 'firemen', and paramedics should be referred to as 'ambulance crews', not 'ambulancemen'.

'Supervisor' is preferable to 'foreman', 'worker' to 'workman' and 'staffing levels' to 'manning levels'.

Remember, over the age of sixteen boys and girls should be referred to as men and women.

A woman who works at home should not be referred to as a housewife.

'Businesses' can be substituted for 'businessmen'.

Be wary of using expressions like 'right-wing', 'left-wing', etc., or describing someone or a group of people as 'extremist'.

Wheelchair users are not 'confined to their chairs', and people with disabilities are not 'the disabled'.

SELF-ASSESSMENT

Location interviewing

- Was the equipment checked and in full working order before I left for the location?

- Was the choice of location relevant to the interview?

- Did I use the location effectively?

- Did I cope with unexpected background noise or interruptions during recording?

- Was the material I collected suitable for the piece I am planning to broadcast?

- Did I leave the location with an interview that was of a high technical standard?

- Did I have problems editing the interview because of intrusive background noise?

- Does the cue sheet provide a good introduction to the final piece?

- What will I do differently next time to improve the quality of my location interview recording?

Studio interviewing

- Did I allow enough time to prepare my guest for the experience of taking part in a studio interview?

- Did the cue material provide an effective introduction to the topic and the contributor?

- Did technical problems disrupt the smooth running of the interview?

- Did my guest enjoy the experience of being interviewed in a studio?

- What will I do differently next time I conduct a studio interview?

Generally

- Did I prepare efficiently for this interview?

- Did I talk too much?

- Was the interview structured correctly?

- Could the questions have been worded more effectively?

- Did I listen to the interviewee and ask questions that developed out of their answers?

- Was I in control of the interview?

- Did I explore the topic sufficiently?

- Was I aware of any other or better stories emerging during the interview?

- What would the listener think of me, the interviewee, the story and the interview as a whole?

9
Analysis of interviews

Taking time to analyse an interview is well worth the effort, no matter what stage you have reached in your interviewing career. Radio listening is about hearing and understanding at first hearing, not rewinding to hear a bit you may have missed. Bear this in mind when you try to analyse a broadcast interview. First, listen to it all the way through and jot down your first impressions. After all, this is how the programme makers expect the listener to hear them. Analysing is more than just listening to the product – whether it is your own work or that of others – and describing what you heard. It involves dissecting the interview into its component parts and deciding what works and what doesn't work for you as a listener. You must then go further and decide why a particular interview works, and compare it to one that you feel doesn't work.

- Try to listen to as many interviews as you can from a wide range of broadcasts.

- Pay particular attention to how the interview is introduced or cued – how the scene is set for the interview. How does the language used in the introduction affect how you listen to the interview?

- Listen to the line of questioning and the order the questions follow.

- Look at the structure of the interview and decide if the questions are answered fully, if there is evasion, or if the interviewer has failed to pick up on any of the replies for further clarification.

- Analyse the purpose of the interview and its place in the bulletin or programme. Is it live or recorded? Has it been edited?

- What clues can you hear that reveal the on-air relationship between interviewer and interviewee? Is it cordial or confrontational? Does the relationship change during the course of the interview?

- Are the interviewer and interviewee speaking with authority? Do you believe what they say? Why? Are the views of the interviewee balanced by the interviewer playing the role of devil's advocate? Can you identify the agenda being followed by the interviewee?

- Notice how the most effective interviews use primary sources. Do you think the interviewee chosen is the right person for the interview? Who would you have chosen to interview?

- Make a point of noting the duration of the interview as a whole and how the time is divided up between questions being asked and replies being given.

- Put yourself in the shoes of the interviewer and then the interviewee. How would you have coped?

- If necessary, transcribe an interview and follow the words as you listen to the original. You will get a clearer idea of how important the tone of voice is to your understanding of what was said, and the role which pauses and stumbles can play in your interpretation of the conversation.

Here are transcripts of a selection of broadcast interviews, some of them well known landmark confrontations, together with the background information to assist you in understanding and appreciating their effectiveness and the impact they would have had on the listener.

BANDA *V* BROWN

In 1962, Dr Hastings Banda of Nyasaland was summoned to Britain by the government to explain some of his activities. He agreed to give an interview to BBC Radio during his visit. At the time Pat Taylor, former Head of Radio Training, was working as a studio manager on the programme *The World at One*. She remembers that the interview was recorded at Heathrow Airport as Banda was leaving the country. It was first broadcast in the 0700 news bulletin on 21 June 1962, and in its entirety on *The World at One* later that day. Banda was obviously used unprepared for interviewer Douglas Brown, who used a polite and persistent line of questioning. Banda could not have been suffering from culture shock, as he had spent some time in Britain and was aware of the ways of our press and media. He was simply determined not to give anything away, and perhaps thought that if he were not to answer any questions then the BBC would not broadcast the interview. He also sounds genuinely surprised by some of the questions being asked. This is one interview which illustrates perfectly just how important it is for the radio listener to hear the questions as well as the answers. Pat Taylor remembers that back at Broadcasting House, Douglas Brown voiced his disappointment with the answers he had received, and was pretty angry about Banda's attitude during the interview. However, everyone involved realised that the interview must be broadcast, because Banda said more by trying to say nothing. You may like to think about who came out on top during this interview.

DOUGLAS BROWN   Dr Banda, what is the purpose of your visit?

DR HASTINGS BANDA   Well, I have been asked by the Secretary of State to come here.

BROWN   Have you come here to ask the Secretary of State for a firm date for Nyasaland's independence?

BANDA   I won't tell you that.

BROWN   When do you hope to get independence?

BANDA   I won't tell you that.

BROWN   Dr Banda, when you get independence are you as determined as ever to break away from the Central African Federation?

BANDA   Need you ask me that question at this stage?

BROWN   Well, this stage is as good as any other stage. Why do you ask me why I shouldn't ask you this question at this time?

BANDA   Haven't I said that enough for any – everybody to be convinced that I mean just that!

BROWN   Dr Banda, if you break with the Central African Federation how will you make out economically?

BANDA   Don't …

BROWN   After all, your country isn't a rich one, is it?

BANDA   Don't ask me that! Leave that to me.

BROWN   Which way is your mind working?

BANDA   Which way? I won't tell you that.

BROWN   Where do you hope to get economic aid from?

BANDA   I won't tell you that.

BROWN   Are you going to tell me anything?

BANDA   Nothing.

BROWN   Are you going to tell me why you've been to Portugal?

BANDA   [*Pause*] That's my business.

BROWN   In fact you're going to tell me nothing at all?

BANDA   Nothing at all.

BROWN   So it's a singularly fruitless interview?

BANDA   Well, it's up to you.

BROWN   Thank you very much.

THE FARMING INTERVIEW

This interview is based loosely on an actual live broadcast. You might like to consider the line of questioning used by the interviewer. What questions would you have asked? Could the questions be re-worded to elicit fuller answers? Did the interviewer pick up from the answers he was being given to determine his next question? What did the listener learn about life on the farm from the interview? Was this a satisfactory interview for the interviewer, the interviewee or the listener?

INTERVIEWER   Before we came on air you were telling me about the jobs you are involved with down on the farm this week, namely lambing, ploughing and harvesting the leeks.

FARMER   Yes that's right. It's a busy time.

INT.   Now, all jobs on the farm are important aren't they? I suppose it would be impossible for you to pick out the most important one, but if you really had to choose one it would depend on the season, wouldn't it?

FARMER   Yes, that's right. But they all have to be done.

INT.   The weather is a big influence on your working day, isn't it?

FARMER   Yes, that's right, but all the lambing is done indoors now.

INT.   You have a lot of sheep on this farm don't you?

FARMER   Yes, that's right. We have one of the biggest flocks in the county and we take on a lot of extra staff to cope with all the work. Mind you, lamb prices at the market have plummeted since last year so we may have to consider reducing our commitment to sheep farming next year and think of an alternative.

INT.   Well that's very interesting but we need to move on as time is running short. You grow a lot of leeks on this farm, don't you?

FARMER   Yes, and they are ready to be lifted now. It's hard work, especially if this cold snap continues.

INT.   And finally, you were telling me earlier that the land may be too wet for ploughing at the moment?

FARMER   Oh, I think it will be OK if the rain holds off tomorrow.

INT.   Thank you very much.

TUNBRIDGE WELLS

In this infamous interview, an elderly, hard of hearing, long-time resident of the town, Alfred Cronwell, was questioned by a lady from the BBC whose clipped tones and aloof air alienated him and failed to elicit any useable answers. Much to the despair of the interviewer, Mr Cronwell was a bit of a handful and deliberately mischievous; and even when a second interviewer, this time a male, tried a couple of questions, he was just as unforthcoming with answers. The names of the interviewers are not on record. I have been assured by many people that the interview was broadcast, but in fact it was not. According to BBC Sound Archives the interview was specially recorded as a demonstration of how not to conduct an interview, and it was used at BBC Radio Training. This interview has been used in features about interviewing and in blooper-type programmes, and has entered the folk memory of broadcasting. I'm sorry to be the bearer of such bad news. Here is a tran-script of a short extract if you have not heard it before. Ask yourself what the interviewer is doing wrong, and how she could have avoided making such a mess of things.

INTERVIEWER   What's the nicest thing about Tunbridge Wells?

MR CRONWELL   What, what?

INT.   What's the nicest thing about Tunbridge Wells?

MR C.   I don't know.

INT.   Don't you know anything nice about it?

MR C.   No.

INT.   Nothing at all?

MR C.   No. I know nothing about Tunbridge Wells.

INT.   But it must be a healthy place.

MR C.   Hmm?

INT.   It must be a healthy place?

MR C.   Oh, it's a healthy place, 'cos you can go back to the fifteenth, sixteenth century, can't you?

INT.   Yes, I ...

MR C.   Perhaps you didn't know that?

INT.   Oh yes, I knew that, but at any rate it must be a healthy place for you to be looking so wonderful at this age.

MR C.   Well, why shouldn't I look wonderful?

INT.   Mmm, well, er, that comes from the inner spirit I know.

MR C.   Hmm?

INT.   That comes from the inner spirit.

MR C.   In a ... ?

INT.   Comes from your own spirit.

Mr C.   I don't know what you want me to say, but if I can say anything to please you I will.

Int.   What you say delights me.

Mr C.   Mmm?

Int.   What you say delights me. I want you to tell me something about living in Tunbridge Wells.

Mr C.   Well I can't tell you. I live in Tunbridge Wells, that's all I can tell you about Tunbridge Wells.

ALICE IN CLUBLAND

This is a transcript of an interview conducted with the owner of a night-club. The interviewer was asked to follow up gossip and accusations of sex discrimination against the owner.

The plan is to make a programme about employment issues and legislation as they affect women in the workplace, and to use this case study as an example of the attitude of some employers towards women. Would you feel happy about broadcasting this interview as it stands? If not, which parts would you consider using? Did the interviewer ask the right questions? Can you ascertain if the interviewer is male or female? Do you think the sex of the interviewer is relevant or important in this scenario? Do you have any concerns about what the listener will think about the interviewee when they hear his answers? Are there any legal concerns that are nagging you about this piece? Why do you think the interviewee agreed to talk to the interviewer? Who else would you want to interview on tape about this particular case study?

Interviewer   Arthur Jackson you, are the owner of 'Nyte Klub' here in Midtown and you have a reputation for employing female staff based on their looks.

Jackson   That's simply not the case. I like to employ staff that are good looking because it makes the place more attractive for the punters, but they have to be good at their job too. To be honest, I prefer to employ barmaids because they do a better job and the punters tell me they like to see a pretty face behind the bar. They do bring in the business and that's what it's all about, but they have to be able to pull a pint.

INT.   Do you tell them what to wear?

JACKSON   Well, I suggest they should look good.

INT.   Why can't they wear clothes that are suitable for the work they do?

JACKSON   It's really about what the punters would like to see a girl behind a bar wearing. It's human nature, isn't it?

INT.   One of your staff told me that she quit her job because you have a very sexist attitude.

JACKSON   I know who you mean. Sharon left of her own accord. She obviously didn't like the way I ran my business, but that's up to her. She's working at the Tavern now and the landlord there insists his girls wear a short skirt or a low-cut blouse.

INT.   I understand that you get a lot of trouble with fights breaking out here – do you think that might be another reason why female staff leave?

JACKSON   It's all part and parcel of working in a club. The door staff are trained to deal with any trouble like that.

INT.   Are your door staff trained?

JACKSON   Yes.

INT.   The police get called out regularly to the club because of fighting don't they?

JACKSON   Listen, I don't know where you get this information, but I can name you three pubs in the town that have much more trouble than we do.

10
Information

BROADCAST JOURNALISM TRAINING COUNCIL (BJTC)

Guidelines for courses seeking accreditation

The BJTC was founded in 1979, as the Joint Advisory Committee for the Training of Radio Journalists, to establish and sustain common vocational standards in the delivery of radio journalism training in universities and colleges in the UK. The Council is representative of those who deliver the courses, the broadcasting industry, the BBC, ITN, IRN, Channel 4, the CRCA and the NUJ, as well as independent broadcasters and those who represent them. These guidelines are a consolidation of the knowledge and experience accumulated individually and collectively by the Council and its members over the years.

The guidelines were revised in 1999 and are intended as an indication to colleges and universities of the basic, minimum requirements to be met by postgraduate diploma, undergraduate and other courses.

The aim of the guidelines is not to produce standardised courses, but to ensure that students receive a sound grounding in the essential skills of broadcast journalism, and that they are equipped on completing their course to take their place in broadcasting newsrooms.

The guidelines indicate what skills practical training should encompass, the role that professional studies should play, technical equipment and resources provision, plus assessment procedure recommendations.

You can read the full guidelines for courses in broadcast journalism, bi-media journalism, and multi-media journalism on the BJTC website (see p.160).

BJTC recognised courses

Postgraduate courses

Bell College of Technology
Cardiff University
City University
Falmouth College of Arts
Highbury College
London College of Printing
Sheffield Hallam University
University of Central England
University of Central Lancashire
University of Leeds, Trinity and All Saints College
University of London, Goldsmiths College
University of Westminster

Undergraduate courses

Nottingham Trent University
The Institute of Communication Studies, Leeds
The Surrey Institute of Art and Design, University College
University of Bournemouth
University of Central Lancashire

There are also a number of further education colleges and training organisations offering a range of courses that will help you obtain formal qualifications like City & Guilds, HNC, HND, SCOTVEC and BTEC. Subjects include radio journalism, radio competencies, radio production and media techniques.

Skillset offers qualifications for anyone who works as a broadcast journalist, reporter, presenter or bulletin editor.

CSV Media offers radio journalism and radio production courses to the unemployed and others.

CROW (Community Radio Open Workshop), Old Phoenix Brewery, 7 Phoenix Place, Brighton BN2 2ND, offers short courses in radio skills.

Some courses offer practical training and study for those wanting to work in the industry as well as bi-media modules which reflect the need for employees with the skills to work in both TV and radio. The demand is now rising for multi-skilled broadcast journalists, particularly within the BBC. You need to be able to research, write, present, interview and have IT skills, plus a clean driving licence. There are also more opportunities for journalists and broadcasters to work as freelancers or on short-term contracts in both national and local radio. The freelance world is very competitive, and the industry needs the flexibility and cost-effectiveness that freelancers can offer.

Take any opportunity that arises to get in front of a microphone. This will help you to understand radio, build your confidence, develop your voice and your presentation skills, and gain that elusive experience to add to your CV, which could make you more attractive in the eyes of editors and will demonstrate to the leaders of courses you apply to that you have a real interest in radio journalism. Experiment with a tape or disk recorder and microphone at home. Try recording yourself reading the weather or some travel information gleaned from your local station. Volunteer to read out the announcements over the public address system at your local fête or show – not exactly radio, but you are communicating with listeners and every bit helps. You could offer your services at the local hospital radio, but be prepared to do anything, as you may have to join a queue of potential presenters. One of the best jobs is recording interviews with patients.

Employers are looking for a genuine interest in and a commitment to radio when they interview candidates for a post. So listen to as much radio as possible and get to understand how it conducts its business. Many broadcasters will tell you that it is necessary to eat, drink and sleep radio in order to be successful in the industry.

RECOMMENDED READING

A *Social History of British Broadcasting*, vol. I, 1922–39, Paddy Scannel and David Cardiff (Blackwell) 1991.
All Our Todays: 40 Years of the Today Programme, Paul Donovan (Jonathan Cape) 1997.

An Introductory History of British Broadcasting, Andrew Crisell (Routledge) 1997.

Broadcast Journalism, Andrew Boyd (Focal Press) 4th edn 1997.

Broadcasting A Life – The Autobiography of Olive Shapley, Olive Shapley (Scarlet Press) 1996.

English for Journalists, Wynford Hicks (Routledge) 2nd edn 1998.

Guide to Independent Radio Journalism, Linda Gage (Duckworth) 1990.

Interviewing Children, Sarah McCrum and Lottie Hughes (Save the Children) 2nd edn 1997.

Interviewing for Journalists, Joan Clayton (Piatkus) 1994.

Local Radio Journalism, Paul Chantler and Sim Harris (Focal Press) 1992.

Making Radio, Michael Kaye and Andrew Popperwell (Broadcast Books) 1992.

McNae's Essential Law for Journalists, Walter Greenwood and Tom Welsh (Butterworth) 14th edn.

Media Ethics, ed. Matthew Kieran (Routledge) 1998.

Producers' Guidelines (BBC) 2nd edn 1993.

Prospero and Ariel: The Rise and Fall of Radio, Lawrence Gilliam (Victor Gollancz) 1971.

Radio Production, Robert McLeish (Focal Press) 3rd edn 1994.

Richard Dimbleby: A Biography, Jonathan Dimbleby (Hodder and Stoughton) 1975.

The Radio Handbook, Pete Wilby and Andy Conroy (Routledge) 1994.

The Spoken Word, Robert Burchfield (BBC) 1982.

Understanding Radio, Andrew Crisell (Routledge) 2nd edn 1994.

USEFUL WEBSITES

BJTC (Broadcast Journalism Training Council) http://www.bjtc.org.uk (information about accredited broadcast journalism courses)

BBC News Online (with bulletins containing audio and video clips, updated hourly) http://www.news.bbc.co.uk

Radio on Demand http://www.bbc.co.uk/radio5live/

BBC World Service News (five-minute bulletin broadcast every fifteen minutes) http://www.bbc.co.uk/worldservice/

Independent Radio News IRN bulletins http://www.irn.co.uk

Radio Academy ('dedicated to the encouragement and recognition of excellence in UK radio') http://www.radacad.demon.co.uk

Broadcasting Standards Commission http://www.bsc.org.uk

BBC Producers' Guidelines http://www.bbc.co.uk/info/editorial/prodgl

News Services:
http://www.ListenToTheNews.com

http://www.pa.press.net (Press Association PA news agency reports)

http://www.wrn.org (live and recorded radio from around the world)

Department of Media, Culture and Sport (including the Group for Broadcasting and Media) http://www.culture.gov.uk

The Presswise Trust http://www.presswise.org.uk

USEFUL ADDRESSES

Central Office of Information (COI) Hercules Road, London SE1 7DU

Department of Sound Records, Imperial War Museum, Lambeth Road, London SE1 6HZ

National Sound Archive, The British Library, 96 Euston Road, London NW1 2DB

Broadcasting Standards Commission, 5–8 The Sanctuary, London SW1P 3JS

Commercial Radio Companies Association, 77 Shaftesbury Avenue, London W1V 7AD

The Radio Academy (and the Student Radio Association), 5 Market Place, London W1N 7AH

The Radio Authority, Holbrook House, 14 Great Queen Street, London WC2B 5DG

BBC, Broadcasting House, London W1A 1AA

BBC Northern Ireland, Broadcasting House, Belfast BT2 8Q

BBC Scotland, Broadcasting House, Queen Margaret Drive, Glasgow G12 8DG

BBC Wales, Broadcasting House, Llandaff, Cardiff CF5 2YQ

Independent Radio News, 200 Grays Inn Road, London WC1 8XZ

The British Forces Broadcasting Service (BFBS), Chalfont Grove, Narcot Lane, Chalfont St Peter, Gerrard's Cross, Buckinghamshire SL9 8TN

Talksport, 76 Oxford Street, London W1N 0TR

Classic FM, 7 Swallow Place, London W1R 7AA

Virgin 1215, 1 Golden Square, London W1R 4DJ
Atlantic 252, 74 Newman Street, London W1P 3LA

Broadcasting, Entertainment, Cinematograph and Theatre Union
   (BECTU), 111 Wardour Street, London W1V 4AY
Institute of Journalists, 2 Dock Offices, Surrey Quays, SE16 2XL
National Union of Journalists, Acorn House, 314–20 Grays Inn Road,
   London WC1X 8DP

Community Media Association, 15 Paternoster Row, Sheffield S1 2BX
Hospital Broadcasting Association, Strathe House, Russel Street,
   Falkirk FK2 7HP
Reporters Sans Frontières, 5 Rue Geoffroy-Marie, 75009 Paris
Women's Radio Group, 90 de Beauvoir Road, London N1 4EN

City & Guilds of London Institute, 46 Britannia Street, London
   WC1X 9RG
CSV Media, 237 Pentonville Road, London N1 9NJ
Skillset, 91–101 Oxford Street, London W1R 1RA

Central Office of Information, Hercules Road, London SE1 7DU
Department of Media, Culture and Sport, 2–4 Cockspur Street, London
   SW1Y 5DH
The Presswise Trust, Easton Business Centre, Felix Road, BristolBS50HE
The Radio Magazine, 25 High Street, Rothwell, Kettering, NN14 6AD
Voice of the Listener, 101 King's Drive, Gravesend, Kent DA12 5BQ

SUGGESTED LISTENING

Audio cassettes

Mark Tulley's India (BBC) reports and interviews by the former BBC
   correspondent
On The Hour (BBC) spoof news with the irreverent Christopher Morris
75 Years of the BBC (BBC) archive material and broadcasting history
Radio Active (BBC) spoof radio programmes from a spoof local radio sta-
   tion, with Angus Deayton
Radio Ballads (BBC) the radio documentaries of pioneering producer
   Charles Parker created between 1957 and 1964, collected on eight
   CDs (Topic Records)

Current output

Radio services in the UK are provided by:

- The British Broadcasting Corporation (BBC), which is responsible for the BBC World Service, the national networks – Radios 1, 2, 3, 4 and 5 Live – regional radio in Wales, Scotland and Northern Ireland, and thirty-nine countywide local stations.

- Independent National Radio (INR), namely Classic FM, Virgin 1215 and Talksport.

- Independent Local Radio (ILR), which at the last count includes over 200 commercial stations.

- Satellite and cable commercial services.

- Community services, including stations broadcasting with RSLs (Restricted Services Licences), hospital and student radio.

More services are promised in the future with the spread of digital radio.

Interviews are featured regularly in a variety of styles and formats on most radio stations in the UK, and are conducted by reporters, producers and programme presenters. Lend an ear to *Today*, *Desert Island Discs*, *You and Yours* and *In Touch* on BBC Radio 4; breakfast and drivetime programmes on BBC Regional and BBC and independent local radio, *The Five Live Report* and *Breakfast with Andrew Neil* on BBC Radio 5 Live, and Anna Raeburn on Talksport. Whatever you choose to listen to, you should be promiscuous and listen regularly to a wide range of interviews and networks. You should be critical and analytical about your listening. Put yourself in the place of the interviewer, the interviewee, the producer and the listener; decide if things could have been done differently, and speculate on the possible results.

More and more stations are starting to put their output on to the internet, so it doesn't matter where you live, you can start to listen to stations even if you are outside their broadcast area. BBC Radio 5 Live has gone one step further by offering *Radio on Demand* on their website, which features highlights and live interviews, together with features and documentaries that they have broadcast, with the option to listen at your own convenience; and for the student of radio interviewing who wants to analyse content and technique, it is possible to download the audio material onto portable players for repeated access and archiving.

TUNING GUIDE

UK frequencies

BBC

BBC Radio 1: FM 97.6–99.8Mhz. Music for youth audience.

BBC Radio 2: FM 88–90.2Mhz. Music and entertainment for mature audience.

BBC Radio 3: FM 90.2–92.4Mhz. Classical music and arts.

BBC Radio 4: FM 92.4–94.6Mhz, LW 198kHz, AM 720kHz. Speech, news and sport.

BBC Radio Five Live: AM 693 and 909kHz. News and sport.

BBC World Service: AM 648 and 198kHz. Wide range of speech and news.

Independent national radio

Classic FM: FM 100–102Mhz. Classical music.

Talksport: MW 1053 and 1089kHz. Chat and sport.

Virgin FM: FM 105.8, AM 1197 and 1215kHz. Music for adults.

Atlantic 252: AM 252kHz. Chart music.

National radio

BBC Radio Wales: AM 882 and 1125kHz (mid-Wales), 657kHz (Clwyd), FM 95.1Mhz (Gwent). English language service.

BBC Radio Cymru: FM 92.0–105.0Mhz. Welsh language service.

BBC Radio Scotland: FM 92.4–94.7Mhz, AM 810kHz.

BBC Radio Ulster: FM 92.4–95.4Mhz, AM 1341kHz 873kHz (Enniskillen).

For the frequencies of local BBC and independent radio stations in the UK, and details of how to access community and cable radio services, check local press or listings magazines.

REFERENCES

Audio archive references

(accessed via the National Sound Archive at The British Library)

They Did it First, BBC Radio 3 (1981): A programme about the documentary radio programmes of the 1930s. Includes extracts from programmes which developed new techniques in the use of actuality, actuality interviews and poetry. Presented by Paddy Scannell and featuring producers Lawrence Gilliam, D. G. Bridson, E. A. Harding and Olive Shapley.

Invitation to Speak: A study of the interview in radio and TV; its uses and abuses. Presented by Leslie Smith (BBC Home Service, 21 June 1961).

I'm Very Glad You Asked Me That (BBC, 13 April 1986): A discussion about the political interview on radio and TV, and the way it has influenced politicians. Presenter: Patrick Hannan.

Written references

'Interviewing on the BBC' (issued to staff in June 1990).
'Practical guide for journalists' (Reporters Sans Frontières, 1996).
Representation of the People Act 1983 (HMSO).
Newspaper and Magazine Publishing in the UK, Code of Practice (ratified by the Press Complaints Commission 26 November 1997).
Radio Authority News and Current Affairs Code (1994).
BBC Sound Archives Chronological Catalogue Volume 1: 1852–1949 (BBC, August 1964).
BBC Handbook 1931 (BBC).
Broadcasting Standards Commission – Codes of Guidance (June 1998).

Glossary

acoustic: the way sound behaves in a particular environment. For example, an empty room with a high ceiling and hard reflective surfaces would have a 'bright' or 'live' sound. The acoustic in a radio studio is specially designed to absorb sound and supply a 'dead' acoustic

actuality: sounds recorded on location either indoors or outdoors

ALC/ARL: Automatic Level Control/Automatic Record Level. A facility on some recording equipment which enables the input level of sound that is being recorded to be adjusted automatically rather than manually by the machine operator

atmos.: atmosphere. The background sounds or ambience that establish the location of a broadcast or recording for the listener, for example the roar of traffic in the street, the echo inside a church, etc. The film term 'wildtrack' is also sometimes used in this context, particularly when referring to sound that is used in a feature, for example, to add atmosphere to the recording

back anno.: back announcement. The words read by a presenter which tell the listener what they have just been listening to

band: one of several inserts on a reel of tape divided up with leader tape between each insert

bulletin: a news broadcast, usually of 2–5 minutes duration, which may contain copy read by a newsreader, interview clips and voicers from reporters

bulk eraser: equipment which generates a magnetic field and is used to 'clean' or 'wipe' tape recordings by re-arranging the magnetic particles on the tape so that it appears to be blank

cans: headphones. Early models of headphones produced such poor-quality sound that they were likened to the communication system favoured by children who used to talk to each other over a short distance by using two tin cans linked by a piece of taut string

cart: cartridge. A plastic container which encloses a tape loop of ¼" tape. Used for short inserts like news clips, wraps, voicers and jingles which are played into bulletins and programmes

clip: a short extract taken from a recorded interview or actuality and used within a news bulletin. Also referred to as a cut

correspondent: a reporter employed by the station or network to cover specialist stories or to report from specific areas or regions

copy: written text of a news story read by a newsreader. Also refers to material provided by news agencies

cue: the written introduction to an interview, package, programme, etc. read by the newsreader, continuity announcer or presenter. Also an instruction to a broadcaster to start speaking

documentary: a mainly speech-based programme which exploits a range of sound material (interviews, readings, poetry, music, sound effects, commentary, etc.) to tell a complicated or multi-layered story, and is based on actuality and contributions from credible witnesses

dub: to make a copy of a recording or transfer recorded material from one tape to another

duration (Dur.): the length of anything to be broadcast in minutes and seconds, e.g. two minutes and forty seconds is written as 2'40"

edit: cutting and splicing together of material on audio tape in order to shorten, remove or re-order the material. The same term is also employed when using digital equipment even though no cutting is carried out. The term 'editing' also refers to the decision-making process used to meet editorial standards

fade: the effect of a sound being gradually reduced to silence

fader: on audio mixing desks, sliding a fader will increase or decrease the sound source allocated to it. Also known as a 'pot' (abbr. for potentiometer)

feature: a produced mode of delivery, usually recorded, which focuses on one subject

feedback: also known as howl-round. A high-pitched tone generated when a sound from a loudspeaker is picked up again by the microphone that originally transmitted it and heard again through the loudspeaker. Feedback can also be generated if a presenter at an open microphone has their headphones turned up too loud, or if the telephone contributor to a live programme has their radio switched on and positioned near the telephone they are using

flip-flop: 1 operational description when broadcast studios on a radio station are used alternately by consecutive programmes; 2 a style of double-headed presentation when links, stories or information are divided up and read alternately by the two presenters

FX: written instruction on a script indicating the use of sound effects

gash (or slash): audio tape removed from a recording and usually thrown away; but longer segments are left on the reel and can be useful for dubbing short clips and recording jingles, trailers and short voice pieces

GNS: General News Service. BBC newsroom which collects and distributes copy and clips to and from national, regional and local newsrooms

gram library: room in which music, sound effects and sometimes audio archive material is stored and accessed at a radio station

grams: refers to the record deck in a studio used to play in music, FX or archive usually stored on vinyl

GTS: Greenwich Time Signal. The pips broadcast to give accurate time checks

headlines: a short summary of the most important news stories in a bulletin

ident: broadcast speech or music in form of a jingle which identifies a radio station on air

ILR: Independent Local Radio. Commercial local radio stations licensed and regulated by the Radio Authority

INR: Independent National Radio. Commercial national radio stations licensed and regulated by the Radio Authority

interview: recorded or live broadcast of conversation between a journalist and contributor. May also be conducted by a researcher to obtain information

interviewee: contributor who answers questions as part of an interview

interviewer: journalist who asks the questions as part of an interview

ips: inches per second. An indication of the speed at which a tape is travelling during a recording or playback. The most common speeds used are 7.5ips (19cm/sec) for recording speech and 15ips (38cm/sec) for music recordings

IRS: Incremental Radio Station. Commercial radio station committed to serving a specific community or minority audience. IRS stations are licensed and regulated by the Radio Authority, and operate within an area already served by an ILR station

ISDN: Integrated Services Digital Network. A service which provides lines to carry broadcast-quality audio from a studio or location to a radio station. The lines are used to carry live broadcasts or to enable interview links which do not feature the crackle of standard telephone lines

leader: coloured non-magnetic tape (so it cannot be used for recording) that is attached to a recorded piece to indicate the start and finish of the recording. It is also used to divide up the separate bands of a tape recording. The most common colour combinations include white, yellow or green at the start; yellow, white or red-and-white-striped for banding; and red to end

levels: the measurement of the loudness of a voice or other sound source. Anyone producing a recording should aim for consistency throughout by taking, setting and monitoring level

link: text that connects an insert, clip or item to others within a package, feature, programme or similar

live: an interview, programme or similar that is broadcast as it is performed, directly to the listener via station output. Can also be used to describe a microphone that is switched on, or any electrical equipment in operation

location: site away from the studio where an interview may be recorded or broadcast live

mixing: the technique of combining or layering separate audio to tell the story. Links, for example, may be read over music or actuality. Successful mixes rely on appropriate levels for each sound source, and effective timings

montage: a feature containing recorded material that is not linked by a presenter or reporter, but tells its story through juxtapositioning of voices, actuality, music, etc.

open reel: a spool of recording tape

outside broadcast: also referred to as an OB. A live or recorded programme or part of a programme broadcast from a location outside the studio

package: 1 a longer and more detailed form of a wrap, in which a reporter packages together links, extracts from interview material, and possibly music and actuality, in a recorded form to tell a story. Successful packages are succinct, focused and creatively produced; 2 IRN, etc. also use the term 'programme package' when they send a wrap to stations

phone-in: the whole or part of a programme that features contributions from listeners on the telephone

popping: the distorted sound of a voice caused by the source being positioned too close to the microphone

pot-cut: to stop the playback of a recorded interview during broadcast at a convenient point by closing the fader, usually at the end of an answer or sentence, before the piece has run its full duration. The decision to pot-cut is usually taken by the producer or editor during transmission, and is usually based on time constraints. Efficient reporters usually make a note on the cue sheet accompanying their piece of any suggested alternative 'out-point' timings

PPM: Peak Programme Meter. A calibrated dial on which the peak recording or playback levels of your piece or programme are indicated by a moving needle and can therefore be monitored during a broadcast or a mix. When told to 'watch your levels' this is what you should be looking at to ensure your output is not so high that it distorts, or so low that it does not register

pre-fade: before committing an audio source to transmission, the levels are checked and adjusted before the fader is opened and the presenter, contributor or recording are broadcast. A facility (a pre-fade switch or gain control) on the mixing desk enables the presenter to play the piece or microphone level and see it on the PPM and hear it in their headphones. The opening seconds of every recording or a few words from a live contributor should be pre-faded before transmission, so that all sound sources sound similar in volume

producer: the person in overall charge of the production or transmission of a live or recorded programme or part of a programme

radio car: vehicle equipped to transmit a signal from a location to the radio station studio enabling a journalist to report live into a programme, conduct an interview, take part in a two-way, or enabling the studio presenter to interview a contributor on site. Also used as part of an OB

recording: the process of collecting and storing sound on audio tape or similar

remote: a small studio into which a contributor to a programme can connect themselves via an ISDN line to the main radio station which may be some distance away. Larger stations will have several remotes dotted around their patch for use by their reporters, correspondents and invited contributors. The studio, the size of a cupboard, will probably be located at a town hall, university campus or similar, where someone can be given the responsibility of ensuring access

ROT: Recording Off Transmission. Recording a live programme for archiving or repeating. An extract or clip from a live interview during a programme could also be used later in a news bulletin

RSL: Restricted Service Licence. A radio service allocated a short-term licence to broadcast for a specific period, and coverage to provide an information and news service to an event like an arts festival, conference or agricultural show

running order: the order of items to be featured in a programme

satellite studio: a fully equipped smaller version of the base station studio. Linked via an ISDN line, it is capable of being used for contributing into the main output of the radio station, but is also available to opt out and broadcast to a specific editorial area. The studio is usually staffed with a small team or just a district reporter or two

segue: pronounced 'seg-way'. A technique used in audio production when consecutive sounds or inserts are mixed directly from one to another without the use of a spoken link

signposting: keeping the listener informed about items or guests that are 'coming up later in the programme'

slug: the catchline at the top of a piece of news copy or cue sheet which identifies the title of the story

soundbite: a short extract taken from a longer interview that differs from an ordinary clip in that it is particularly effective in summing up an opinion, experience, situation or feeling

splice: another word for an edit in a tape recording

splicing tape: the white adhesive tape used for joining edited audio tape

talkback: an off-air system that enables a producer or technical operator in a control room or studio to speak to the presenter in a studio on headphones during a broadcast and on loudspeaker when the microphone is off

TBU: Telephone Balance Unit. Studio equipment that matches the levels of the studio presenter's microphone with that of a telephone contributor

tone: a single continuous note played into the mixing desk by a studio engineer or technician and used to align and set the standard level of all the audio broadcast equipment in the studio

top-and-tail: to attach colour-coded leader tape at the start and end of an interview if it is recorded on audio tape

two-way: an interview between a programme presenter and correspondent or reporter. Also an interview where the interviewer and the interviewee are in different but linked studios

Uher: a make of portable open-reel tape recorder

voice piece: also known as a voice report or voicer. A reporter or correspondent reads their scripted report during a news bulletin or programme via the phone, on tape or down the line from another studio

vox-pop: a selection of short comments voiced by the general public in response to a question and recorded by a reporter in the street before being edited together montage-style

wrap: a scripted voice report which also includes one or two clips of illustrative audio

Index

accuracy 145–6
Acheson, Fran 50
acoustics 55, 61, 91
actuality 55, 89–92
Adie, Kate 36
administration 137
ALC/ARL (Automatic Level Control/Automatic Record Level) 54
Alos, Donna 50
Analysis 123
angles 6

back announcement 140–1
Banda, Hastings 149–51
BBC: *Handbook* 1–3; history 2, 4, 5; *Producers' Guidelines* 20–1, 28; radio training 50, 152; sound archive 4
bi-media 47
BJTC (Broadcast Journalism Training Council) 156–7, 160
BNP (British National Party) 24
Breakfast with Andrew Neil 163
Bridson, D.G. 165
Brooke, Louisa 49–50
Brown, Douglas 149–51
BSC (Broadcasting Standards Commission): broadcasting standards bulletin 23–5; Code of Practice 39–40; Codes of Guidance 41, 42
bulk eraser 62–3

Call Nick Ross 124
Callaghan, Jim 15
Campbell, Nicky 14, 104
Canal Journey 3
Carter, Sidney 4
Century Speaks, The 47, 118

Clegg, Julian 45–6
clichés 11, 144
clips 9, 114, 136–7
COI (Central Office of Information) 44
concealed recordings 29, 41
Contempt of Court 37
correspondents 5, 9, 48–9, 103–4
courses 156–8
cues 137–41

Day, Robin 14, 16
Desert Island Discs 12, 119
Dimbleby, Richard 4
discussions 2, 22–3, 127–8
documentary 10, 111–12
Dolley, Philippa 43–4
doorstepping 29–30, 39–40
Dunn, John 14

editing 22, 28, 29, 31, 133–7
embargoes 30, 65
ethics of interviewing 24–31
exercises 11–13, 54–6, 69–70, 76, 79, 83–4

features 9, 112–3
first impressions 85–6
Five Live Report, The 163
focus 66
Freeman, John 14
Fuller, Russell 47–8

Gilliam, Lawrence 3, 165
Graham, Natalie 47
grammar 144
Gretton, David 4

Hannan, Patrick 165
Harding, E.A. 165
Hayes, Brian 124
Heath, Edward 105
Holme, Lord 41
Home Truths 120
Humphreys, John 14

I'm Very Glad You Asked Me That 15, 165
In the Psychiatrist's Chair 12
In Touch 163
In Town Tonight 2
interviewees: choosing 22, 68–70; difficult 95–100; getting the best out of 94–5; need to know 22, 70–2; role 18
interviewer: role 13–14; types 14–18, 49
interviewing: BBC 20–1; children 38–9; criminals 37–8; demonstrators 40–1; interpreters 110–11; live 86–8; location 89–94; people in authority 30, 39–40, 104–6; personalities 39–40, 45–6, 107–9; public 39–40, 106–7, 123–5, 128–31; recorded 88–9, 92–3; relatives and friends 12–13, 109–10; sensitive 26–8, 30, 43–4
interviews: agreeing 8; as live 120–1; categories 10–11; planning 66–8; refusing 8, 40; successful 7, 11; using 9–10
Invitation to Speak 14, 165

Jenkins, Brian 44–5

Lawley, Sue 14
levels 54, 90, 92
libel 31–4
listening, suggested 162–4
Littlemore, Sue 48–9
Live From London 120
Lloyd, Helen 46

magazine programmes 10, 119–20, 122–3
media scrums 102–3
meeting and greeting 86
Metropolitan Police 40
microphones 58–9, 90, 119
Midweek 120
montages 9–10, 113–14
Murray, Jenny 14
music 117, 137
My Century 118

National Sound Archive 4, 165

Naughtie, James 14
NUJ: code of conduct 19–20

'Opping 'Oliday 3
oral history 46–7, 117

packages 9, 115–17
Paxman, Jeremy 105
personal safety 35–7
phone-ins/phone interviews 10, 42, 60, 123–5
playback 31, 93, 133
popping 59, 92
portable recorders 52–8
presentation 141–3
press conferences 100–2
press releases 64–6, 83–4
Presswise Trust 40
pronunciation 145

questions: asking 79–81, 119; types 81–3

Radio Authority: conduct of interviews rules 22–3
radio car 59–60, 94, 126–7
Radio on Demand 163
Raeburn, Anna 163
reading aloud 141–3
recording 52–8, 79, 88–93
Redhead, Brian 105–6
references: audio 165; written 165
Reith, Sir John 2–3
Reporters Sans Frontières 35
Representation of the People Act (1983) 34–5
research 7, 49–50, 72–6
retakes 132–3
risk assessment 76–9
Rowinski, Paul 50–1
running order 122–3

safety precautions 63
self assessment 146–7
Scannell, Paddy 165
scenarios 28–31
Shapley, Olive 3, 165
Smith, Leslie 165
sources 64–6, 149
Speed the Plough 3–4
sport 47–8
Standing on the Corner 2
studios: radio station 52, 61–3, 86; remote 60, 125–6; satellite 125–6

Talk Radio 23 -5
Talks Department 1–2, 4
taster 9
Taylor, Pat 149–50
Tebbit, Norman 15
Thatcher, Margaret 105–6
They Did It First 2–3, 165
They Speak for Themselves 3
time management 68
Today 12
Todd, Chris 49
Tunbridge Wells 152–4
tuning guide 164
20th Century Vox 118
two-ways 9, 48

violence 36–7
vocabulary 143–6
vox-pops 9, 10, 128–31

Whale, James 23
Wilson, Harold 105
Woman's Hour 43
World at One, The 149
World Tonight, The 49
wraps 9, 115
writing 137–41

You and Yours 163
Young, Jimmy 14